BELONGING

A Guide for Group Facilitators

Self and Social Discovery for Children of All Ages

Written by

Jayne Devencenzi

and

Susan Pendergast

Illustrated by
Linda Lyon - Wright

Words Processed by
Carol Cauley

Belonging: San Luis Obispo, CA

Published by: BELONGING
                     2960 Hawk Hill Lane
                     San Luis Obispo, CA   93401

First Edition
Second Printing, 1990

ISBN 0-9623822-0-5

Copies of this book may be ordered by sending $19.95 plus $2.00 for shipping and handling (CA residents add $1.20 sales tax) to:

                     BELONGING
                     2960 Hawk Hill Lane
                     San Luis Obispo, CA   93401

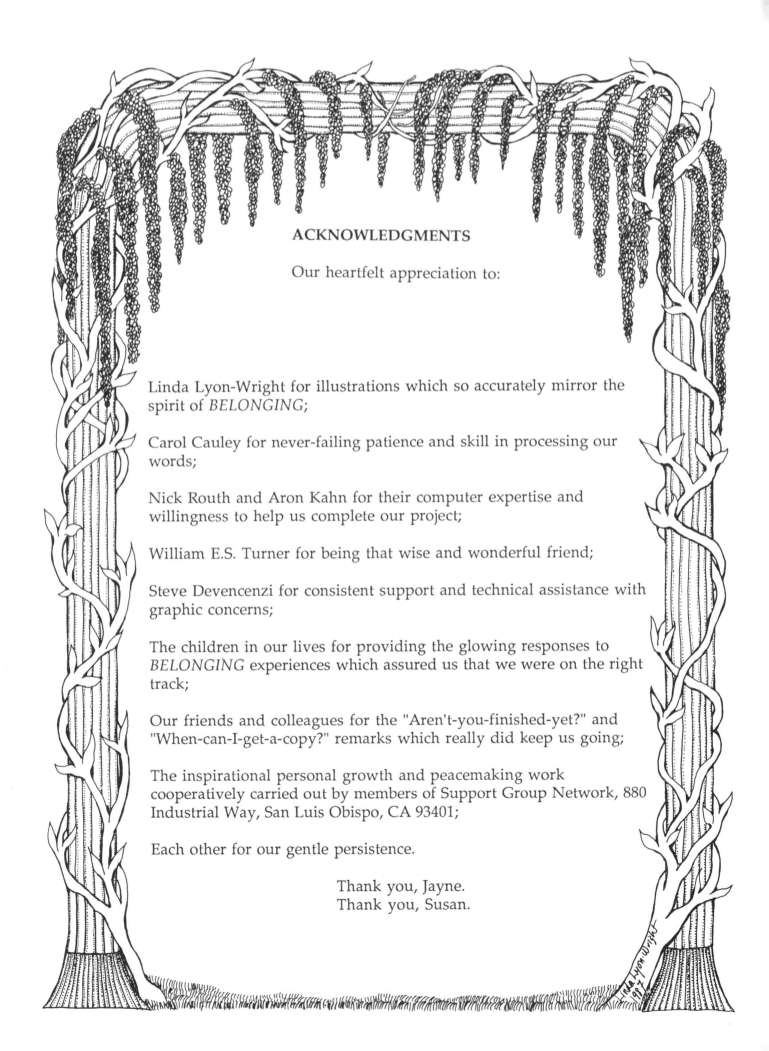

ACKNOWLEDGMENTS

Our heartfelt appreciation to:

Linda Lyon-Wright for illustrations which so accurately mirror the spirit of *BELONGING*;

Carol Cauley for never-failing patience and skill in processing our words;

Nick Routh and Aron Kahn for their computer expertise and willingness to help us complete our project;

William E.S. Turner for being that wise and wonderful friend;

Steve Devencenzi for consistent support and technical assistance with graphic concerns;

The children in our lives for providing the glowing responses to *BELONGING* experiences which assured us that we were on the right track;

Our friends and colleagues for the "Aren't-you-finished-yet?" and "When-can-I-get-a-copy?" remarks which really did keep us going;

The inspirational personal growth and peacemaking work cooperatively carried out by members of Support Group Network, 880 Industrial Way, San Luis Obispo, CA 93401;

Each other for our gentle persistence.

Thank you, Jayne.
Thank you, Susan.

To...

Celebrants of the human experience...
that we might be reminded of our
connections and return to a peaceful
state of being, flowing with, belonging
with each other, and all that is.

-- J. D.
S. P.

Linda
Lyon-Wright
1987

CONTENTS

Beginning . . .

Beginning...

According to a wise and wonderful friend, human beings need two things from one another: to be touched and to be heard. When these needs are met, people experience a sense of belonging. All seems right with the world.

While working with children of all ages, we meet many who retreat from human interactions and many who burst loudly upon others. They all miss the desired connection: no one comes near and no one listens. Watching them and sensing a reawakening of the vulnerable child in ourselves, we attempt to create a safe environment in which these young people learn skills to deal successfully with people and, thus, acquire that sought-after sense of belonging.

BELONGING evolved from years of interactions with people and our mutual struggle to create a workable system through which to learn important People Skills. We have practiced labeling and disclosing feelings, giving and receiving information, supporting the efforts of others and accepting different perspectives. We have explored our personal strengths and weaknesses and have made contracts for positive change. We have focused on mistakes we all make and the importance of recovering from them and reducing the stress in our lives. We have allowed others to participate with us cooperatively and have trusted a group of friends to help us solve problems. Together we seem to smile and laugh more, pat ourselves on the back more, risk more. We celebrate life more fully.

And so what? So we have a bunch of celebrating people. Do we achieve more? Are fewer "dropping out"? Are we having an effect on the incidence of substance abuse or delinquency? *BELONGING* is a practitioner's guide for facilitating the acquisition of People Skills. The intent is not to quantify data or address the hypotheses implied in those questions. Our educated guess is "yes" to all of the above. Our hearts lead us to say that we don't care about those projections as much as we are attracted to the vision of a peaceful young person who has the personal power and social confidence most of us have been in search of for a lifetime.

We heard "through the grapevine" about each other's work with children and immediately connected with each other. We blended our knowledge and styles to refine a process and series of experiences. Simultaneously, we agreed that our efforts needed to be documented and given to others inspired to help children of all ages grow socially and emotionally. We are motivated by the fact that we know ours is a quality program to be shared and, more selfishly, by the need to know that a circle of facilitators is growing to provide support for us and our belief that we are "heart and soul" as well as "mind and body." We invite those who have a desire to work with children of all ages, a commitment to model the tools taught, and the courage to be an equal risk-taker with others to join us...to belong.

Carry on...

Learning the
Process

Linda Lyon-Wright
1987

Chapter 1

Learning the Process

The group process provides a structure through which People Skills, things everyone needs to know in order to get along with self and others, are explored. The system was originally designed for children eight through fourteen years of age. However, the process has been used effectively with older populations, including adult support and parenting groups. In addition, exceptional children, those with extraordinary learning and/or emotional needs, have responded well to the process. For each group of four to eight members, at least one adult facilitator is needed. Ideally, forty-five minutes twice weekly is made available for the group experience. A comfortable, quiet environment is most conducive to successful group functioning. Group members are seated in a circle. Chairs or pillows help define space boundaries for group members.

A graphic presentation of the group process used in *BELONGING* is located on the following page. Displaying this visual representation of the process in poster form is helpful when teaching and learning the format for each group meeting.

Choose a Leader

Share a Social Time

Share a Feeling Sentence

Process Steps

Give and Receive Compliments

Present a Problem or an Activity

Share Ideas

STEP 1: CHOOSE A LEADER

Every group meeting begins with the selection of a leader, who is the adult facilitator, in the early stages of the group's life. Over time and depending upon the sophistication of group members, the facilitator determines when others are ready to serve as facilitators for all or part of a meeting. Some guidelines for determining when this transition occurs include:

1.   The adult facilitator leads the group for at least three or four beginning sessions until members feel at ease in the group.

2.   After these initial meetings, a selected group member shares leadership with the adult facilitator by directing steps two and five (**Share a Feeling Sentence** and **Give and Receive Compliments**).

3.   When everyone understands the process and operating instructions, a member who brings a problem to the group serves as the facilitator for steps three and four (**Present a Problem or an Activity** and **Share Ideas**).

4.   When group time is used for direct teaching and practicing of a new People Skill, the adult assumes the facilitator role.

5.   The goal is for everyone to experience being the facilitator. Reluctant group members are provided with a nonthreatening exercise to lead in order to assure success.

STEP 2: SHARE A FEELING SENTENCE

The first task of the chosen facilitator is to ask all group members, moving from person to person around the group, how they are feeling. One purpose of this step is to focus members' attention on each other. Another purpose is to identify any negative feelings brought to the group and determine the problems related to those feelings. The structure used for stating feelings is modeled by the facilitator until its use is automatic: "Today I feel_____ because _____" or "Right now I feel_____ because _____." The facilitator has the additional task of being a reflective listener and restating what each group member says. For example, "It sounds as if you feel_____ because _____" or "I heard you say that you feel _____ because _____." As the group begins, all words and reasons are acceptable as long as they fill the blanks in the model sentence. Initially, the leader makes suggestions only if someone says, "I feel like doing _____," instead of using a feeling word. For example, "Right now I feel like cutting class because I can't do the work." In this case, the facilitator acts as a guide by giving several feeling words from which to choose and by asking the member to restate the feeling sentence. To complete the example given, the facilitator says, "Do you think you feel sad, angry or confused?" After a word choice is made, the leader asks the member to state, "Right now I feel angry because I can't keep up in that class." Over time a great deal of energy is spent on learning to label and disclose feelings, as this is an essential People Skill. These opening feeling statements become clearer and more specific with practice. The connections between events, thoughts, and resulting feelings become more apparent. Repeatedly, emphasis is placed on owning one's feelings.

STEP 3: PRESENT A PROBLEM AND/OR AN ACTIVITY

Now that the group is aware of everyone's presence and feeling state, the group experience moves in one of two directions: (1) solving a problem brought to the group or (2) learning and practicing a new People Skill. The facilitator needs to be prepared to direct activities centering on a specific People Skill and equally prepared to abandon the activity in favor of working through a problem with a group member. Many times both problem solving and skills work happen in the same session. The more People Skills are practiced, the more realistic the problem solving will become.

When group members bring problems to the group, they are responsible for stating the problem to the rest of the group. Before the group has practiced the problem-solving model presented in chapter 10, "Solving Problems," the adult facilitator guides members in taking ownership of their problems. For example: If someone says, "I don't like him," the leader asks the member to restate the problem: "I don't like it when _____." The individual sharing the problem calls on those offering help with the solution.

STEP 4: SHARE IDEAS

While members are learning the process, sharing ideas is encouraged after someone presents a problem and during activities. The sharing of ideas is not a part of the other process steps. For example, group members are encouraged not to react verbally to feeling statements and compliments, except to say "Thank you."

In the beginning, the facilitator emphasizes:

1. An exchange of ideas requires a listener as well as a speaker. Reference is made to the behaviors used by an active listener presented in chapter 11, "Sharing Ideas."

2. Ideas offered in the group are to be constructive. The Operating Instructions Chart, addressed in the last paragraph of this chapter, serves as a reminder that put-downs are not acceptable. The refinement of these skills is considered in chapter 11, "Sharing Ideas."

STEP 5:   GIVE AND RECEIVE COMPLIMENTS

The ability to give and receive compliments with ease is characteristic of an assertive person.   When learning the process, group members are asked to compliment, to say something positive about someone in the group.   The facilitator especially needs to encourage compliments related to something someone said or did in group, as opposed to how someone looks or general statements about character.   For example, "Tony, I like your shirt" and "Angela, I think you are nice" are redirected by the facilitator: "Can you also think of something special they did or said in group today?" "Tony, I like the way you looked at me when you had something to say" and "Angela, I appreciated your suggestion about my problem" are more personal.   In addition, compliments given to individuals as opposed to the entire group tend to be more powerful.   For example, "Bill, I appreciated the way you smiled at me when I came into the room" has more impact on an individual than "You all were nice to me today."

Often, receiving a compliment is more difficult for people than giving one. A good practice is to identify to whom the compliment is given before saying it.   For example, "Shirlee, I have a compliment for you, OK?" This gives the receiver a chance to refuse if getting a compliment is uncomfortable at first.   Group members are told that the response to a compliment is "Thank you" and nothing more. Also, members are encouraged to let a compliment "soak in" before giving one to someone else.

STEP 6:   SHARE A SOCIAL TIME/CLOSURE

This step is particularly useful when focusing group efforts on the People Skill of "Having Comfortable Conversations." Group members sometimes choose to bring snacks to share. After a few minutes of eating and conversation, closure is achieved in children's groups by having everyone pile hands on top of the hands of others in the center of the circle, by having everyone join hands around the circle and give a squeeze, or by patting someone on the back. Some groups are more comfortable with touching than others are. Individuals may choose to hug each other upon leaving. If physical contact is a sensitive issue within a group, a word of closure is used instead, such as "It was great to be together" or "This is a really special group," etc.

OPERATING INSTRUCTIONS

While learning the process, emphasis is placed upon following the operating instructions of the group. Behavioral guidelines are most effective when the group has ownership of them. Brainstorming expectations is one of the group's first tasks. The Operating Instructions presented here are suggested by the facilitator as part of the brainstorming process. Frequent referral is made to the **Operating Instruction Chart**. Without interrupting the flow of the group process, the facilitator points to a behavior to remind a group member of expectations.

Some groups require more work on learning to conform to behavior expectations than others do. For these groups, special techniques may help and are used as the group participates in introductory inclusion exercises. One system, tried successfully with young children, uses a group member as a behavior monitor. This person monitors other group members for compliance with group expectations. The designated individual taps the one who is not accepting responsibility for having appropriate behavior and then tells the group the ignored guideline. If the same one is responsible for breaking a rule again, that person may be asked by the group to leave for a brief time to return when the group consensually agrees.

In order for the process to have any meaning, there has to be a group within which to apply it! "Forming a Group" presents procedures for identifying group members, guidelines for grouping, suggestions for dealing with changes in group composition, and qualities necessary to be an effective group facilitator.

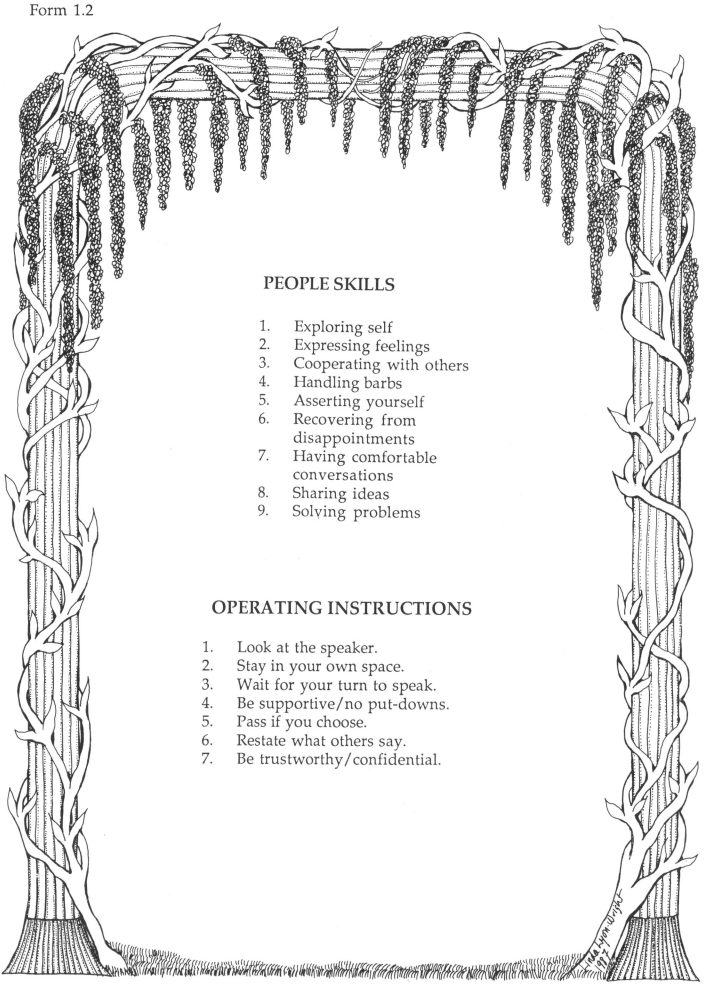

PEOPLE SKILLS

1. Exploring self
2. Expressing feelings
3. Cooperating with others
4. Handling barbs
5. Asserting yourself
6. Recovering from disappointments
7. Having comfortable conversations
8. Sharing ideas
9. Solving problems

OPERATING INSTRUCTIONS

1. Look at the speaker.
2. Stay in your own space.
3. Wait for your turn to speak.
4. Be supportive/no put-downs.
5. Pass if you choose.
6. Restate what others say.
7. Be trustworthy/confidential.

FACILITATOR LOG

Things to remember:

_____

_____

_____

_____

_____

_____

_____

_____

_____

_____

_____

_____

_____

_____

_____

_____

_____

_____

_____

_____

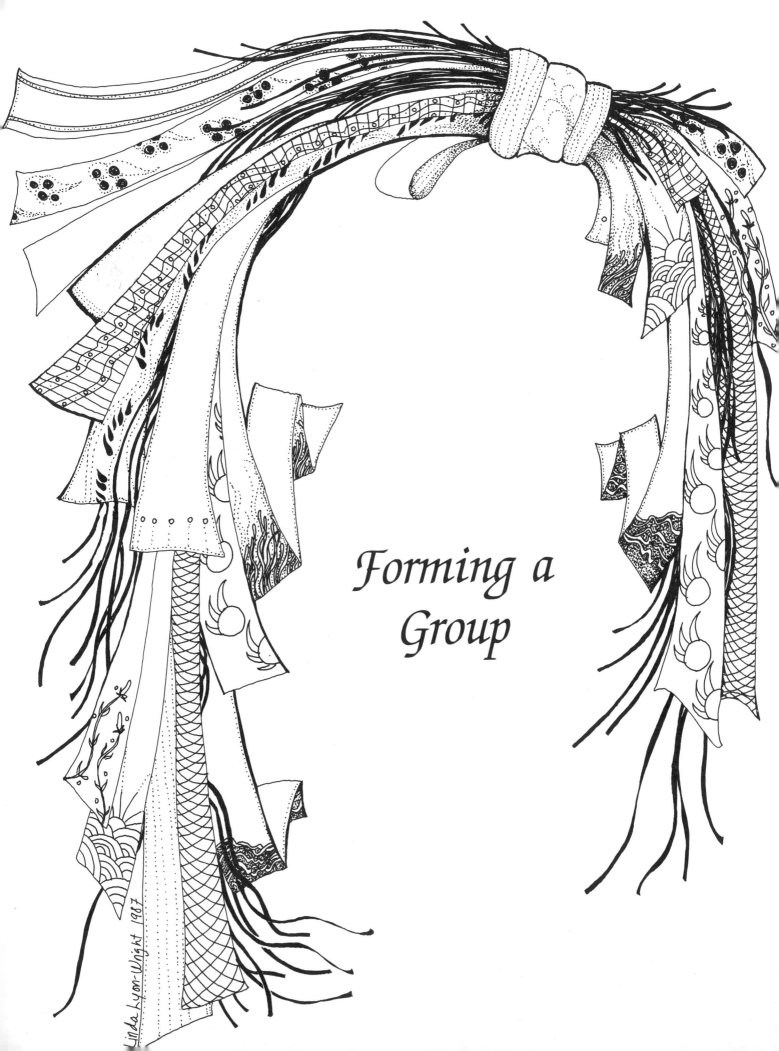

Forming a
Group

Chapter 2

Forming a Group

This group process has been piloted in a variety of settings. Procedures have been created to identify those young people with particular life adjustment needs who could benefit from a structured social skills program and the opportunity to learn how to successfully interact in a group. The process is also used to guide normal social development and is useful in varied settings: support groups for children, parent groups, rehabilitation programs, as well as other unlimited possibilities.

The following suggestions for organizing a new group are particularly applicable to school settings. Forms and letters are adapted to meet the needs of a particular situation. The proposed member identification system developed for use in schools allows for staff, parent and self referrals. Staff members fill in short referral forms which include simple guidelines for selecting students in need of assistance and a section for commenting on areas of concern (Form 2.1). All parents for a given school site are sent information about the social skills groups offered, either in personal letters or in school newsletters. Conferences are held to follow up on any resulting parent referrals (Form 2.2). Young people are informed of groups available to them in classroom presentations carried out by the group facilitator (Form 2.3). A drop box is provided for students to leave confidential notes of request for involvement.

When initial referrals are received from parents or staff, either party or both are asked to complete a behavior checklist to give more information about a given child (Form 2.4). The items on the checklist are directly related to the content of the People Skills which are dealt with in group. The checklist gives information to the group facilitator about areas of unique concern for individuals as well as areas of common concern among group members.

In a follow-up conference, those who have been assertive enough to make self-referrals are asked to complete a self-survey to give the group facilitator more information about how skilled they perceive themselves to be (Forms 2.5, 2.6). Information from the surveys serves as a basis for discussion with individuals and as a guide to help with grouping. With the young person's permission, significant adults are asked to fill out the behavior checklist, too. A comparison is made between how the potential group members sees themselves and how others see them. The confidentiality of self-referrals is always respected.

Deciding upon the composition of any group is a formidable task. Facilitators review the information obtained about a given set of young people and consider grouping those with similar problems. If the common characteristics are passive or shy/withdrawn in nature, a larger group (seven - eight) maximizes the possibilities for verbal exchange. If the behavior pattern of the group tends to be aggressive/acting-out in nature, smaller groups (four - five) are optimal. Including several more socially capable individuals in the group is helpful. Their behavior serves indirectly as a model for other group members.

Besides common problem distinctions, age/maturation level and gender are considered. No more than a two- to three-year age span is recommended when working with children. When deciding whether to group children with age-level and older peers or age-level and younger, maturational factors are considered and a judgment call made. For instance, a fourteen-year-old with limited social skills might feel threatened in a group of age peers and might progress more rapidly with a younger group. As a rule, males and females are grouped together to encourage communication without gender considerations. A balanced number of males and females in a group permits equal comfort and support. However, there may be specific instances in which a facilitator opts for an all-male or all-female group.

The most significant factor in forming a group is obtaining the consent of the individual to participate. Contracts are sometimes used to offer reinforcement for trying the group for several sessions before committing to membership (Form 2.7). Potential members are simply and honestly told the purpose of the group and how it might benefit them. If persons are receptive and communicate easily during this first meeting, they are asked to fill out the same self-survey used with self-referrals. Group participants are told that the surveys will help each see personal growth in the group.

Since the facilitator is a key member of the group, the qualities of an effective leader deserve careful consideration. Some desired traits include:

1. **A willingness to make a time commitment to the group experience of at least nine to twelve months** (unless the group decides to conclude earlier). Making a trust connection with children/people and then reneging can be devastating, hindering the chances for future trust relationships.

2. **An understanding of the operating instructions for a successful group, especially confidentiality.** All group members, including the facilitator, respect the privacy of the group and divulge group information only with prior consent.

3. **An abundant history of life experience with children either as a parent or in a paraprofessional/professional capacity** (applies to facilitators of children's groups). When facilitating children's groups, the ability to connect with the child in one's adult self is helpful. Experiencing life through the eyes and ears of a child is more easily accomplished by people who frequently spend time with children/young adults.

4. **A personal warmth as demonstrated by a good expressive vocabulary of feelings and a sensitivity to emotional needs.** In short, prospective facilitators consider how approachable they are. Is the facilitator comfortable dealing with emotional issues? Is this person a good listener?

5. **An open-minded outlook toward new information about human behavior.** Persons who see life, including their own, as a process or journey are the most effective leaders.

6. **The ability to express oneself in a simple, organized manner.** The facilitator's role is not one of lecturer. All verbal input is short and concise, with active participation of all group members.

7. **An acceptance of the facilitator's role as guide and not judge.** Effective leaders are nonjudgmental, pointing out options without labeling them right/wrong or good/bad.

8. **The ability to model People Skills in one's own life.** When group members see the leader doing the behaviors focused on in group, they are more apt to understand and try the new skills. Modeling is a powerful learning tool.

Over the course of time spent with a group, the composition may change for a variety of reasons, such as someone moving or people opting to discontinue involvement. As much as possible, the facilitator avoids having members leave during a conflict. Members are encouraged to work through conflict first before deciding to leave or stay. Also, unless a group dwindles to fewer than four, keeping the original members without additions is most comfortable. The group requires time to adjust to the loss of a member before new members are added. Any change in composition results in a change of group dynamics and interrupts the group process. This doesn't have to be viewed as negative, since being flexible enough to handle changes is an important part of the People Skill of "Recovering from Disappointments." A change in group composition is used as a learning experience for the group.

When a group is beginning or when new members join an existing group, energy is focused on developing feelings of belonging and trust within the group. The following chapter, entitled "Launching a Group," contains a series of nonthreatening, get-acquainted exercises to build group cohesion and safety.

PEOPLE SKILLS
STAFF REFERRAL

The social skills groups I will be facilitating have the goal of learning "People Skills," i.e., things one needs to know in order to get along with self and others. We will be learning about:

1. our own strengths/weaknesses
2. feelings: how and when to express them
3. cooperating with others
4. handling negative interactions
5. being assertive
6. giving and receiving information
7. relaxing and recovering from mistakes and disappointments
8. having comfortable conversations
9. solving problems

If you have someone to refer for involvement in a group, please fill out the lower portion of this form and return it to me.

Sincerely,

PEOPLE SKILLS
STAFF REFERRAL

Student_____Comment_____

_____

Student_____Comment_____

_____

Student_____Comment_____

_____

Teacher_____Date_____

Linda Lyon-Wright 1987

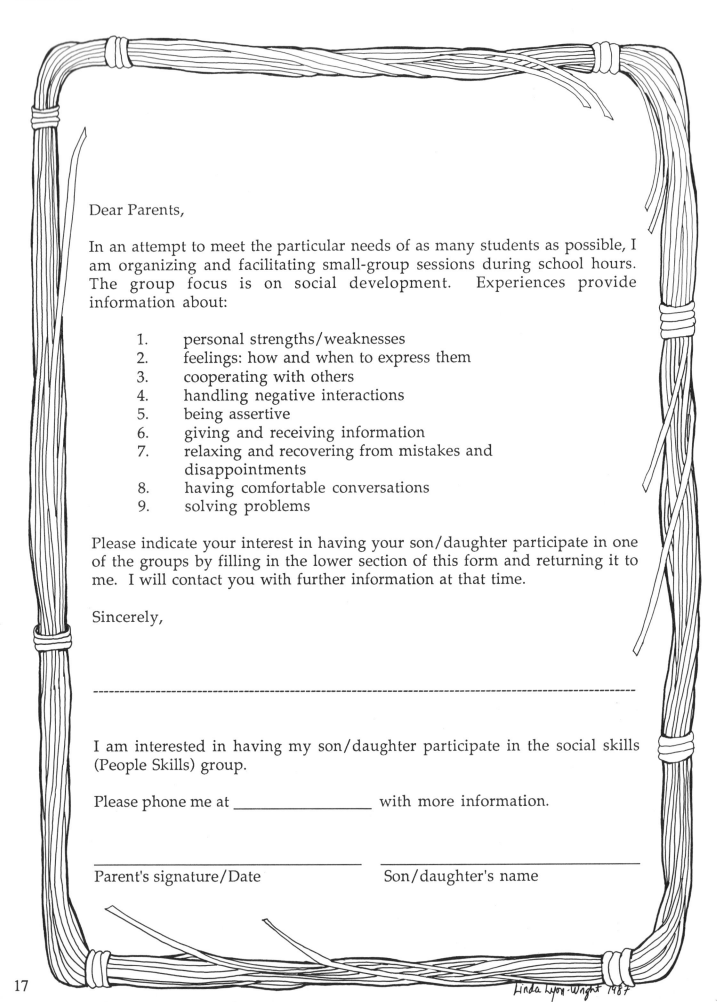

Dear Parents,

In an attempt to meet the particular needs of as many students as possible, I am organizing and facilitating small-group sessions during school hours. The group focus is on social development. Experiences provide information about:

1. personal strengths/weaknesses
2. feelings: how and when to express them
3. cooperating with others
4. handling negative interactions
5. being assertive
6. giving and receiving information
7. relaxing and recovering from mistakes and disappointments
8. having comfortable conversations
9. solving problems

Please indicate your interest in having your son/daughter participate in one of the groups by filling in the lower section of this form and returning it to me. I will contact you with further information at that time.

Sincerely,

I am interested in having my son/daughter participate in the social skills (People Skills) group.

Please phone me at _____ with more information.

_____   _____
Parent's signature/Date   Son/daughter's name

Linda Lyon-Wright 1987

Hi!

I will be meeting weekly with small groups of students, 5-8 at a time. The purpose of these groups is to learn more about people and relationships. Some areas we will explore include:

1. personal strengths/weaknesses
2. feelings: how and when to express them
3. cooperating with others
4. handling negative interactions
5. being assertive
6. giving and receiving information
7. relaxing and recovering from disappointments
8. having comfortable conversations
9. solving problems

If you would like to belong to a group and share your ideas with others, complete the lower part of this form, tear it off, and put it in the drop box outside my office. I will get back to you and will keep your involvement confidential.

Thanks,

Yes, I would like more information about the groups you've described. Please contact me.

_____

Name

_____   _____

Teacher   Date

Linda Lyon-Wright 1987

BEHAVIOR CHECKLIST

Student's Name_____ Grade_____ Date_____
Name of person completing form_____
Relationship to child_____

Rate each of the listed behaviors according to how well it describes this
child:

(1) not at all   (2) moderately well   (3) very well

			(1)	(2)	(3)
ES	1.	is pleased with own accomplishments	( )	( )	( )
ES	2.	knows own strengths and weaknesses	( )	( )	( )
EF	3.	expresses needs and feelings appropriately	( )	( )	( )
EF	4.	is comfortable giving and receiving affection	( )	( )	( )
CO	5.	is well-behaved	( )	( )	( )
CO	6.	is well-liked by peers	( )	( )	( )
HB	7.	thinks before acting	( )	( )	( )
AY	8.	approaches new experiences confidently	( )	( )	( )
AY	9.	defends own views under pressure	( )	( )	( )
SI	10.	accepts criticism well	( )	( )	( )
SI	11.	is a good listener	( )	( )	( )
RD	12.	can accept things not going own way	( )	( )	( )
RD	13.	adjusts well to changes	( )	( )	( )
CC	14.	expresses ideas willingly	( )	( )	( )
SP	15.	resolves own peer problems	( )	( )	( )

Please describe any other pertinent behavior:

_____

_____

_____

KEY:
ES-Exploring Self   SI-Sharing Ideas
EF-Expressing Feelings   RD-Recovering from
CO-Cooperating with Others   Disappointments
HB-Handling Barbs   CC-Having Comfortable
AY-Asserting Yourself   Conversations
SP-Solving Problems

Linda Lyon-Wright 1987

SELF-SURVEY I

Name_____

Grade_____Age_____ Date_____

CIRCLE THE ANSWER THAT BEST DESCRIBES YOU.

| *ES | 1. | I get along with other kids. | Yes | Sometimes | No |

| *EF | 2. | I tell people how I feel. | Yes | Sometimes | No |

| *HB | 3. | I share my ideas even if someone laughs at me. | Yes | Sometimes | No |

| *EF | 4. | I like to agree with my friends. | Yes | Sometimes | No |

| *AY | 5. | I have trouble asking for things. | Yes | Sometimes | No |

| *CO | 6. | I like to play games with others. | Yes | Sometimes | No |

| *CC | 7. | I enjoy talking with people. | Yes | Sometimes | No |

| *RD | 8. | I get upset when things don't go my way. | Yes | Sometimes | No |

| *SP | 9. | I know what to do when I have a problem. | Yes | Sometimes | No |

| *ES | 10. | I can do things well when I want to. | Yes | Sometimes | No |

----

* See key on Form 2.4.

Linda Lyon-Wright 1987

SELF-SURVEY II

Name_____

Grade_____Age_____ Date_____

			Always	Sometimes	Never
*ES	1.	I get along well with others.	( )	( )	( )
*EF	2.	It's easy for me to share my feelings with others.	( )	( )	( )
*HB	3.	I share my ideas even when someone laughs.	( )	( )	( )
*SI	4.	It's important for friends to agree with each other.	( )	( )	( )
*AY	5.	It is difficult for me to tell people what I need or want.	( )	( )	( )
*CO	6.	I like to get together with friends.	( )	( )	( )
*CC	7.	It's hard for me to talk to people.	( )	( )	( )
*RD	8.	I spend a lot of time thinking about mistakes I've made.	( )	( )	( )
*SP	9.	I ask people to help me solve problems.	( )	( )	( )

COMPLETE THE FOLLOWING SENTENCES.

*ES 1. The thing I do best is _____.

*EF 2. Today I am feeling _____.

*HB 3. When someone is rude to me, I _____.

*SI 4. I know people are listening to me when they _____

_____.

*AY 5. When I need help, I _____.

*CO 6. When someone in charge gives me a direction, I feel_____

_____.

*CC 7. When I meet someone new, I _____.

*RD 8. When things don't go my way, I _____.

*SP 9. When I have a problem, I _____.

* See Key on Form 2.4.

Linda Lyon-Wright 1987

GROUP PARTICIPATION CONTRACT

I agree to participate in a People Skills group for several sessions to see how I like it. Then I will decide whether or not I want to continue.

Some things I would like to learn:

1. _____

2. _____

3. _____

_____   _____
Participant 's Signature   Date

- -

I agree to assist you in the group. Some ways I can help:

1. _____

2. _____

3. _____

_____   _____
Facilitator's Signature   Date

Linda Lyon-Wright 1987

FACILITATOR LOG

Things to remember:

_____
_____
_____
_____
_____
_____
_____
_____
_____
_____
_____
_____
_____
_____
_____
_____
_____
_____
_____
_____
_____
_____
_____
_____

Launching a
Group

Chapter 3

Launching a Group

In the beginning of a group's life, the facilitator guides members through inclusion or get-acquainted exercises. By participating in the following introductory activities, members may, and hopefully will, (1) find the group a safe and fun place to be, (2) see themselves as belonging to the group, and (3) begin to trust other group participants enough to make some simple, self-disclosing statements. The facilitator selects activities appropriate for a given group and returns to them as a source of renewed energy when needed.

I. NAME GAME -- to get acquainted and have fun

OBJECTIVE

Group members will volunteer to participate in a humorous, nonthreatening activity.

MATERIALS

None

PROCEDURE

The facilitator begins by telling group members that they will be playing a name game. No specific directions are given. Members listen to the facilitator's example and then volunteer to participate. First is the facilitator's own name, followed by a mode of transportation, and a place. Each item stated starts with the first letter in the person's first name. For example: "My name is Fred. I drive a Ferrari. I'm from France."

II. **TREASURE HUNT** -- to get acquainted and begin to disclose personal
information

OBJECTIVE

Group members will interact to gain knowledge about each other.

MATERIALS

"Treasure Hunt" sheet (Experiences 3.1, 3.2), pencils

PROCEDURE

Members are given a "Treasure Hunt" sheet (Experience 3.1 or 3.2). They are asked to find others who fit the descriptions on the worksheet. When members find people who fit an item, those persons sign their names in the appropriate spaces. More than one person may sign the same item. Members may sign their own sheets once. After completing the Treasure Hunt, members share things learned. The format is appropriate for any age and is easily adaptable to particular themes or issues, such as family history, relationships, and work experience.

TREASURE HUNT #1

Find someone who:

1. knows how to ride a horse. _____

2. doesn't have any brothers. _____

3. wears the same size shoe as you do. _____

4. has a job and likes it. _____

5. speaks two languages. _____

6. has an older sister. _____

7. has a birthday in the same month as you do. _____

8. has a living great-grandparent. _____

9. knows how to make an omelet. _____

10. has been to a foreign country. _____

TREASURE HUNT #2

Find someone who:

1. is an only child. _____

2. has a computer. _____

3. has a collection of some kind. _____

4. enjoys bike-riding. _____

5. lives in an apartment. _____

6. likes to cook. _____

7. has experienced divorce. _____

8. has been backpacking. _____

9. loves to read. _____

10. has the same color of eyes as you do. _____

III. SHARING SECRETS -- to begin to disclose information

OBJECTIVE

Group members will share one item of personal information with the rest of the group.

MATERIALS

One 3"x5" card for each group member, pencils

PROCEDURE

Group members write a secret about themselves on a 3"x5" card. They do not put their names on the cards. They are to write something they wouldn't mind sharing with others. For example, "I'm afraid of the dark." After all cards are completed, members drop their "secrets" into a bag. When all the cards are in the bag, members take turns selecting a card from the bag and reading it aloud. If the activity is done with young children or those having learning problems, it is helpful for the facilitator to read the cards. Everyone tries guessing to whom the secret belongs. When all cards have been read and secrets disclosed, participants discuss how they felt when sharing secrets.

IV. **THE WEB** -- to get acquainted with each other

OBJECTIVE

Members will share information about themselves with the group and be able to remember one item someone else shared.

MATERIALS

A ball of yarn

PROCEDURE

Group members sit on the floor in a circle. The facilitator holds onto the end of a ball of yarn and states something personal. The yarn is then passed to group members, who also hold onto the yarn and state something about themselves. As the yarn moves from person to person, a web is formed. Members get a visual picture of how they are joined together as a group. Members are asked to try to remember what someone else said.

Suggested topics, moving from nonthreatening to self-disclosing, include:

1. If you could be an animal, what would it be?
2. What is something you do well?
3. What do you enjoy doing in your spare time?
4. What is your favorite color, song, place, food, etc.?
5. Who is someone important to you? Why?
6. What is something you wish for or hope to do?

When facilitators are working with children's groups, maintaining contact with parents by informing them of topics discussed or progress made in group is an effective means of encouraging communication at home. A regular information exchange, providing the child agrees, includes statements of a general nature, i.e., "Mary's group is working to understand the importance of trust among group members" (Form 3.3). Group members need to feel certain that notes home aren't going to reveal confidential information. While the intent is not to conceal information from parents, a child's right to privacy is respected and confidential information is not revealed without prior consent. If the group leader and child want to share, a conference is scheduled with parent, facilitator, and child.

The facilitator leaves these opening exercises when group members are heard saying, "When's our next meeting?", "This is fun," or "I like it here...." From that point on, the challenge is recognizing, practicing and mastering People Skills. The facilitator refers to the self-surveys and behavior checklists to determine which People Skill to approach first. A universal starting place is self-exploration. Hence, the next chapter, "Exploring Self."

HOME/GROUP INFORMATION EXCHANGE

Dear _____,

Today in group we talked about _____

_____

_____

_____

_____

_____

_____

This memo is to keep you informed. Please contact me with any questions or concerns.

Sincerely,

_____

Facilitator

_____

Phone Number

Linda Lyon-Wright 1987

FACILITATOR LOG

Things to remember:

Exploring Self

Chapter 4

Exploring Self

Self-exploration happens when people journey inside themselves to discover more about who they are as individuals. One desired outcome of the experiences included in this section is a greater degree of self-awareness. From this improved self-knowledge springs increased self-acceptance. Both lead to a secure belief in unlimited potential for growth: an appreciation, celebration of self. Over time, members are guided to see that higher degrees of self-awareness, self-acceptance, and appreciation of self provide a solid foundation upon which positive, meaningful interactions and connections with others occur.

The activities in the following chapters are divided into **Awareness**, **Practice** and **Transfer** phases. Each level is progressively more demanding, requiring that group members assume more responsibility for their own development. Members retain self-exploration materials in personalized scrapbooks/journals. After completion of the "Exploring Self" activities, group members review each person's scrapbook/journal and comment on things remembered most, new information learned, and feelings about the experiences.

I. **PURPOSE** -- to increase self-awareness, acceptance, and appreciation

Hot Seat

AWARENESS

OBJECTIVE

All group members will receive positive messages about themselves from other group members.

MATERIALS

Tall stool or chair, slips of paper, timer, felt pens or pencils

PROCEDURE

Group members write their names on slips of paper and give these to the facilitator. From the collected papers the facilitator chooses one name. The chosen person sits on the stool or "hot seat" and listens as group members "bombard" the individual with positive comments. Statements made are in sentence form or, to speed the input, just one-word items, i.e., "kind," "smart," "polite," etc. Having a list of suggested descriptive words on display helps get the process started. One group member keeps time as the spotlighted person takes in the information for one minute. The "hot seat" person is then directed to say "Thank you" and nothing more. The leader guides the process by encouraging eye contact, relaxed body posture, no verbal reactions to what is said, and a continual flow of positive information.

Brag Session
PRACTICE

OBJECTIVE

Group members will state a continuous flow of positive information about themselves.

MATERIALS

Tall stool or chair, slips of paper with names on them, timer, felt pens

PROCEDURE

The facilitator chooses a person randomly by drawing a name. This person sits on the "hot seat" and begins to relate personal strengths to the group. A group member times the process for one minute. (The time is gradually lengthened as the activity is repeated in future sessions. A five-minute session would be a realistic and desirable goal.) The facilitator provides a format to follow, such as "I am a person who _____" or "I can _____." The facilitator redirects someone who says, "I think I can" to say, "I can _____." During each person's minute the facilitator interjects new formats, such as "Now, just say single words which describe you." This is helpful if the person is having difficulty coming up with self-statements. The activity, for such people, is altered so that they write self-statements for one minute and then read them or have them read. As with any activity, anyone may pass.

Pride In Self

TRANSFER

OBJECTIVE

Group members will write a positive statement about themselves.

MATERIALS

Pride Sheet (Experience 4.1)

PROCEDURE

At the end of the group meeting, the facilitator gives each member a Pride Sheet and asks members to fill it out before the next group meeting. Members bring the completed sheet to the next meeting, where they are asked to share some of their pride statements.

Pride Sheet

This pride sheet belongs to _____

I am proud of myself because I _____

_____

I am proud because I did _____

_____

I am proud to have said _____

_____

I am proud to have_____ for a friend.

I am proud because I can _____

I am proud to be _____

II. **PURPOSE** -- to look at one's life to date

Family Tree
AWARENESS

OBJECTIVE

Group members will complete a Family Tree Chart indicating those people they consider to be part of their family or to be significant others.

MATERIALS

Family Tree charts (Experience 4.2), pencils or felt pens and chart paper or chalkboard and chalk

PROCEDURE

The group begins with a discussion of how each person defines family. For each member the facilitator records the definition, which will be referred to when the activity is completed. All participants are given a Family Tree chart and directed to write their own names on the trunk and fill in the names of those perceived as being part of their family, according to personal definitions. Many do not live in a traditional family structure. All members are encouraged to view their family systems as unique and not strange or unacceptable. Completing the tree with names of significant others gives safety to the adopted or foster child who may wish to do two trees or combine groups on one. When the trees are complete, group members read their definitions of family and share their trees. The facilitator ends the activity with the question, "How is our group like a family?" This leads to a broader discussion of the need to belong.

Family Tree

Lifeline

PRACTICE

OBJECTIVE

Group members will relate a one-minute autobiography.

MATERIALS

Lifeline (Experience 4.3), pencils, timer

PROCEDURE

Group members consider highlights of their lives to date. Each writes notes about these on the "Lifeline" sheet. When this is complete, all members are given two minutes each to relate important elements of their lives to the rest of the group. Additional time is given for questions group members may have for the person who's sharing.

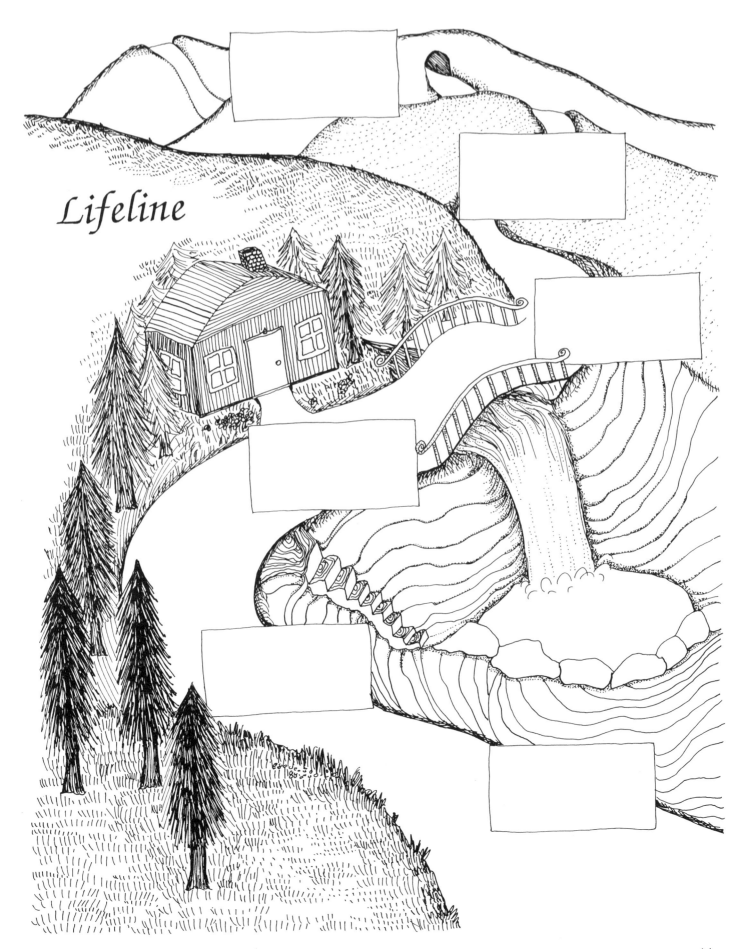

Lifeline

Cooperative Story

TRANSFER

OBJECTIVE

Group members will share significant life events from birth to present age by creating a cooperative story.

MATERIALS

None

PROCEDURE

The facilitator begins the exercise by taking one minute to tell a significant personal experience about birth and instructs the next person to tell something which happened at several months of age. The next person picks up the story by adding an event from the first year of life. Each person in turn takes one minute to contribute an experience from increasing ages. The story appears to be about one person who is really a composite of everyone present.

A sample story might read:

Facilitator: I was born prematurely in an emergency room in a hospital in Boise, Idaho.

Person 2: When I was three months old, I was in Mexico City with my family. We lived there until I was two years old. I spoke both English and Spanish.

Person 3: When I was two years old, my twin sisters were born. I remember feeling very left out, but my grandfather paid special attention to me.

Person 4: I cut off all of my hair when I was three. My mother cried and cried and taped ribbons on my head....

The story continues until the "composite person" reaches the age of the youngest group member.

Last Person: On my eighteenth birthday, I went on a solo hike in the Sierras. I kept a journal of my experiences and self-discoveries.

III. **PURPOSE** -- to increase self-awareness, acceptance and appreciation

NOTE: Journals will be used in transfer activities throughout the People Skills program after their function is established here. Children especially relate to the idea of having an "empty book" to be "filled up" with their thoughts and feelings in words and pictures.

Journals In History

AWARENESS

OBJECTIVE

Group members will discuss the concept of empty books/journals and brainstorm possible uses for them. **

MATERIALS

Journals (cloth-bound, spiral-bound, handmade)

PROCEDURE

The facilitator directs a discussion about the history of diaries and journals. The focus is on how they have been used historically or traditionally.

1. How were diaries and journals used in the past? (Documentation of travels, explorations, wars, personal feelings)

2. Can you think of any examples of famous diaries/journals? (*The Diary of Anne Frank*, etc.)

3. Why would a contemporary person choose to write in a diary/journal?

4. What would you like to do with your journal? What kinds of things will you include?

==
** Inspired by and adapted from *The Creative Journal: The Art of Finding Yourself*, Lucia Capacchione, Swallow Press, Athens, Ohio, 1979.

Journal Writing Exercises
PRACTICE

OBJECTIVE

Group members will complete a self-awareness exercise to begin journals.

MATERIALS

Journals, pens, pencils, felt pens

PROCEDURE

The following is a list of topics to be used during group sessions over a four- to five-week period.

1. Tell or draw about your likes and dislikes.

2. Draw or tell about someplace you'd really like to go. Tell or show who would go with you.

3. Think back in time. Draw or write a vivid memory you have of either a pleasant or unpleasant event.

4. Draw or write an ending for these unfinished sentences:

LEVEL I	LEVEL II
At school I....	After high school, I....
Friends are....	Friends are....
I know how to....	A good relationship is....
I like it when....	I am happiest when....
Sharing is....	I really know how to....
My family....	Family is....
I am smart when I....	Being smart is....

5. Make a list or draw about things you would change if you could. Take three minutes to do this.

6. Describe or draw a favorite daydream.

7. List five things you would never change about yourself.

8. If I could be anything I wanted to be, I would....

9. One thing about myself I'd really like to change is....I'll start changing by....

10. I wish that I....

11. Write a thank-you note to someone in your past.

12. Describe a relationship that ended or changed. How did you feel?

13. Describe or draw someone who is very special to you. Tell why that person is so special.

14. One way I deal with loneliness is....

15. Plan at least one special treat for yourself each day of the week. Write these down. Example:

    Sunday -- Play softball with John.
    Monday -- Go for a walk by myself.
    Tuesday -- Buy myself a frozen yogurt.

Journal Writing - Metaphor

TRANSFER

OBJECTIVE

Group members will write about themselves as an object in nature.

MATERIALS

Journals, pencils, pens

PROCEDURE

As an outside assignment, group members are asked to select an object in nature, such as a tree, rock, stone, or blade of grass and to write about themselves as if they were that object. Members may also choose to draw what they would look like being the object. Members write in their journals describing in detail what they see around them and how it feels to be that object. They expand this daily by writing down something they imagine experiencing as this object. Information is shared with the group at its next meeting.

IV. PURPOSE -- to encourage group members to identify and affirm their personal strengths and to use affirmations and visualizations to achieve desired change

Developing Affirmation Statements

AWARENESS

OBJECTIVE

Group members will write and practice affirmations.

MATERIALS

Affirmation Cards (Experience 4.4), pencils

PROCEDURE

The facilitator explains to members that affirmations are positive statements people make to and for themselves or others. The group discusses real-life examples of how negative "self-talk" brings negative results and how affirming oneself has positive results. Group members make lists of five to ten **realistic** goal statements. Some examples include:

1. I will get more things accomplished.
2. I will be friendly to those I meet.
3. I will value and love myself.
4. I will learn how to study for tests.

After this, members write affirmations using their goal statements. Affirmations are **positive, first-person, present tense, action** statements, such as:

1. I am an action person. I finish what I start and I know I do it well!
2. It is like me to be warm and friendly when I meet others, and I know others respect me for it!
3. I am a valuable, lovable person, and I succeed in what I do!
4. I am a person who studies well for tests, and I am rewarded with good grades!

Group members **read** affirmations to themselves or to the group. They are encouraged to repeat affirmations frequently and with much emotion.

"I am a person who _____

_____

_____."

"It is like me _____

_____

_____."

"I am _____

_____

_____."

Picturing Affirmations

PRACTICE

OBJECTIVE

Group members will state affirmations, draw pictures about the affirmations, and experience in their imaginations the end result desired from their affirmations.

MATERIALS

Affirmation Cards made in the previous awareness experience, drawing paper, crayons or pens, chalkboard

PROCEDURE

Facilitators post the following equation which is a helpful tool for teaching the significance of affirming oneself and visualizing new behavior:

POSITIVE SELF-TALK + IMAGINING + REAL PRACTICE = PERSONAL ACHIEVEMENT OF DESIRED GOAL

(affirmations, appreciations)   (visualizing, practicing in your head)

Group members are instructed to read their affirmations. Members decide whether or not they have the **real skills** required to achieve the desired end result of the affirmations. If not, the group brainstorms ways to **obtain** and **practice** the needed **real skills**. When members are certain they have necessary real skills and plan to actually practice (with supervision, if possible), the facilitator instructs the group on the significance of **practicing in the imagination**.

Group members draw pictures of themselves doing the action desired from their affirmations. The use of bright colors is encouraged in the drawings. Next, members are instructed to study their pictures, close their eyes and try to imagine themselves as seen in the drawings. The facilitator explains that this is "visualizing" and that imagining oneself doing a desired behavior is a powerful means of acquiring that behavior.

Affirm & Visualize

TRANSFER

OBJECTIVE

Group members will generate an affirmation independently, practice saying it, and visualize themselves doing the desired behavior.

MATERIALS

Blank Affirmation Cards made in previous awareness activity

PROCEDURE

The facilitator instructs group members to write an affirmation at home and to say it at least twenty times daily. Group members are reminded to practice the real skills needed to achieve the desired end and to visualize themselves successfully doing the selected behavior. Members are encouraged to report progress to the group and to keep affirmations posted or in file boxes.

The process of self-exploration is lifelong. By returning to self-study exercises and reviewing journals throughout the People Skills program, the facilitator demonstrates to group members that lives are journeys, rarely static and usually changing. Emotions associated with the continual flow of human experiences are the subject of the next section, "Focusing on Feelings."

FACILITATOR LOG

Things to remember:

_____

_____

_____

_____

_____

_____

_____

_____

_____

_____

_____

_____

_____

_____

_____

_____

_____

_____

_____

_____

_____

Focusing on
Feelings

Linda Lyon-Wright 1987

Chapter 5

Focusing On Feelings

Members are encouraged to practice identifying and disclosing feelings throughout the People Skills training. Sharing a feeling statement is a constant component of each group experience. The ability to express one's own feelings and interpret how others feel contributes greatly to success with all other People Skills. For example, disclosing strong feelings around a disappointment reduces the time it takes to recover from that disappointment. Acknowledging the fact that one is nervous about carrying on a conversation eases anxiety and promotes more comfortable conversations. Letting people know positive feelings one has for them increases cooperative interactions, and properly interpreting feelings of others reduces conflicts.

The following series of activities was selected to help people learn to read verbal and nonverbal cues in order to accurately label their own feelings and the feelings of others. The experiences provide practice in how and when to express feelings and teach group members an expanded vocabulary of feelings. The activities also give practice in making "I" statements to demonstrate ownership of feelings. The final set of experiences allows for creative exploration of feelings with colors.

I. **PURPOSE** -- to help group members determine how others are feeling by observing their body language

Emotional Postures

AWARENESS

OBJECTIVE

Group members will demonstrate certain feeling states through movement. Group members will label feelings based on body posture.

MATERIALS

None

PROCEDURE

Group members practice:

1. sitting erect
2. sitting slumped with head back and legs crossed
3. sitting slumped with head down and hands folded
4. sitting erect, pulling back with face covered
5. standing erect with feet apart and arms folded
6. standing with legs apart and arms up in the air
7. standing with arms pushing away
8. standing with head back and hand on chin
9. sitting slumped with arms crossed and tapping foot
10. standing with body completely limp

The leader guides members to identify how people might be feeling when their bodies are held in these ways. The examples sighted could represent:

1. proud
2. relaxed
3. sad
4. frightened
5. angry
6. surprised
7. disgusted
8. thoughtful
9. mad
10. depressed

The facilitator creates other postures to be tried and encourages the use of synonyms for commonly used feeling words.

Feeling Movements

PRACTICE

OBJECTIVE

Group members will move in ways that depict a variety of emotions.

MATERIALS

Feelings Vocabulary sheet (Experience 5.1)

PROCEDURE

The facilitator whispers a feeling to a group member who then moves in a way which demonstrates that emotion, such as a depressed walk or an excited jump. Others in the group identify various feelings which could relate to the movement. Members discuss the appropriateness of attaching a particular feeling word to the demonstrated movement.

Linda Lyon-Wright 1987

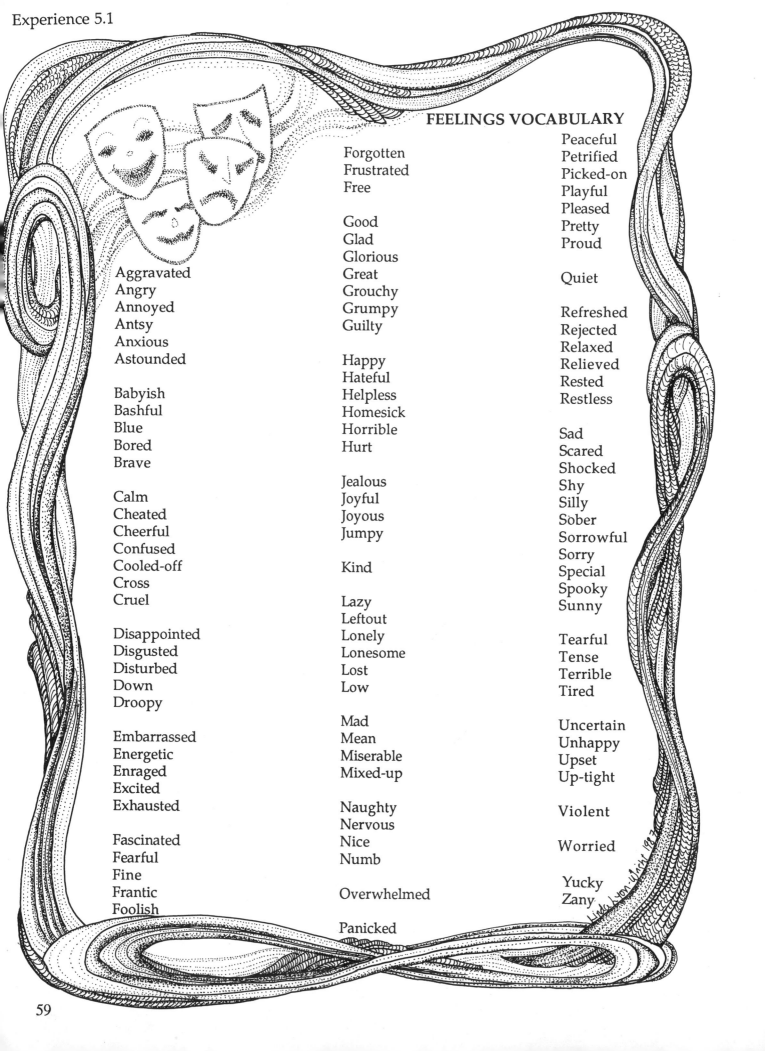

FEELINGS VOCABULARY

Forgotten
Frustrated
Free

Good
Glad
Glorious
Great
Grouchy
Grumpy
Guilty

Happy
Hateful
Helpless
Homesick
Horrible
Hurt

Jealous
Joyful
Joyous
Jumpy

Kind

Lazy
Leftout
Lonely
Lonesome
Lost
Low

Mad
Mean
Miserable
Mixed-up

Naughty
Nervous
Nice
Numb

Overwhelmed

Panicked

Aggravated
Angry
Annoyed
Antsy
Anxious
Astounded

Babyish
Bashful
Blue
Bored
Brave

Calm
Cheated
Cheerful
Confused
Cooled-off
Cross
Cruel

Disappointed
Disgusted
Disturbed
Down
Droopy

Embarrassed
Energetic
Enraged
Excited
Exhausted

Fascinated
Fearful
Fine
Frantic
Foolish

Peaceful
Petrified
Picked-on
Playful
Pleased
Pretty
Proud

Quiet

Refreshed
Rejected
Relaxed
Relieved
Rested
Restless

Sad
Scared
Shocked
Shy
Silly
Sober
Sorrowful
Sorry
Special
Spooky
Sunny

Tearful
Tense
Terrible
Tired

Uncertain
Unhappy
Upset
Up-tight

Violent

Worried

Yucky
Zany

Journal Writing - Body Language

TRANSFER

OBJECTIVE

Group members will complete journal exercises concerning "reading" body language.

MATERIALS

Journals, pens

PROCEDURE

Group members describe how someone they care about looks when that person is feeling:

1. ignored
2. miserable
3. cheerful

Members write what event occurred and what others might have thought before they demonstrated this feeling. During the next group session, members share their entries and tell how **they** look or act when experiencing the feelings described.

II. **PURPOSE** -- to help members accurately label their feelings

Feelings Collage
AWARENESS

OBJECTIVE

Group members will complete a cooperative feelings collage and label the emotions depicted.

MATERIALS

Magazines with pictures of people, glue, butcher paper

PROCEDURE

The facilitator directs group members to cut out pictures of people whose body language/facial expressions demonstrate a variety of feeling states. These are glued onto butcher paper until it is completely covered. Group members take turns identifying the feelings represented and are encouraged to consider synonyms for common feeling words. For example, angry could be irritated, aggravated, or furious. The collage is saved for the next session.

For a group of young children, the facilitator labels several feeling words on the butcher paper, i.e., angry, excited, lonely, or happy, and asks the children to find pictures that illustrate the specific feeling words. They glue the pictures next to the appropriate feeling word.

Feelings Continuum
PRACTICE

OBJECTIVE

Group members will brainstorm synonyms for common feeling words.

MATERIALS

Feelings Continuum drawn on butcher paper (see model below), the collage from the previous session, felt markers

---

FEELINGS CONTINUUM

Angry	Sad	Afraid	Bored	Calm	Happy	Silly
1.	1.	1.	1.	1.	1.	1.
2.	2.	2.	2.	2.	2.	2.
3.	3.	3.	3.	3.	3.	3.
4.	4.	4.	4.	4.	4.	4.
5.	5.	5.	5.	5.	5.	5.

PROCEDURE

A group member serves as a recorder as others brainstorm words which could be used in place of the feeling words at the top of the continuum. New words are listed in the proper category. The feelings collage from the previous meeting serves as a stimulus for expanding word choices. A list of feeling words is included to assist the facilitator in the activity (Experience 5.1). The continuum of expanded vocabulary and the collage are left posted to help group members become more specific with their use of feeling words.

Journal Writing-Exploring Feelings
TRANSFER

OBJECTIVE

Group members will complete open-ended sentences.

MATERIALS

Journals, list of open-ended sentences for each group member
(see list below)

PROCEDURE

The facilitator asks group members to respond to each of the following sentences
prior to the next meeting by writing the sentences and responses in their journals:

1. When I'm feeling _____,

   I show it by _____.

2. Sometimes I show people how I feel by

   _____.

3. I'm feeling _____ because I

   _____, and I would like to

   _____.

4. I feel angry when _____.

5. I worry about _____.

III. **PURPOSE** -- to help members learn to take responsibility for their feelings

"I Feel..." Statements

AWARENESS

OBJECTIVE

Group members will complete and restate sentences to make
"I feel...." statements.

MATERIALS

Sentence examples (included below)

PROCEDURE

The facilitator gives all group members a sentence orally and asks them to either complete it or restate it, using "I feel...." as the opening. The progression of sentences given below moves from simple to complex in terms of the independent thinking required.

LEVEL I

Complete:

1. When a boy/girl says hello to me, I feel _____.
2. When a boy/girl asks me to play, I feel_____.
3. When I get money for doing a chore, I feel _____.
4. When I am working for money, I feel _____.
5. When I help a friend, I feel _____.
6. When I ask for help, _____.
7. When I don't understand something, _____.
8. When I like people, and they don't like me, _____.
9. When my sister/brother uses my things, _____.
10. When I go somewhere I really like, _____.

LEVEL I

Restate:

1. I watched a scary movie last night.
2. My teacher never calls on me in class.
3. Grandma came to visit and brought me a surprise.
4. My class is going on a field trip tomorrow.
5. Doug and Shannon wouldn't let me play soccer with them at recess.
6. I twisted my ankle and fell in the cafeteria.
7. I'm not allowed to play with my friend Kathy.
8. My bike is old and rusty.
9. David always finishes his work before I do.
10. My friend asked me to spend the night.

LEVEL II

Complete:

1. When a boy/girl says hello to me, I feel _____.
2. When a boy/girl asks me out, I feel _____.
3. When I am working for money, I feel _____.
4. When someone stares at me, I feel _____.
5. When I help a friend, I feel _____.
6. When I ask for help, _____.
7. When I don't understand, _____.
8. When I like people, and they don't like me, _____.
9. When my sister/brother uses my things, _____.
10. When I'm dressed up to go out, _____.

LEVEL II

Restate:

1. I went to a horror movie last weekend.
2. Mr. Brown always reads Carol's work to the class.
3. My grandmother took me shopping and bought me a lot of new clothes.
4. The French Club is going to Paris this spring.
5. I was eliminated from the basketball team.
6. I twisted my ankle and fell in the cafeteria.
7. Jane's parents won't let us see each other.
8. This shirt is old and ugly.
9. Jack always finishes his exams before I do.
10. Paul held my hand on the way home.

Role Playing Feelings

PRACTICE

OBJECTIVE

Students will own their feelings by rephrasing sentences, making them "I feel...." statements.

MATERIALS

Role-play Scripts (Experiences 5.2, 5.3)

PROCEDURE

The facilitator reiterates that people often hide their feelings and/or pretend they belong to someone else by not claiming them with the simple word "I." Group members are given the role-play situations. A pair acts out the script as is and then attempts to restructure the wording, using "I feel...." statements. For example:

Jill: I've been curious about why you didn't try out for honor band.

Kim: Oh, it makes me too nervous to play alone in front of others.

Restated:

Jill: I've been curious about why you didn't try out for honor band.

Kim: Oh, I feel too nervous playing alone in front of others. I felt afraid to audition.

ROLE-PLAY SCRIPTS FOR "I FEEL...." SENTENCES
LEVEL I

SCENARIO 1

Karen: What are you doing this weekend?
Sarah: My mom makes me so mad! She makes me do all of my chores before I can play.

SCENARIO 2

Jason: Do you want to come over and play Saturday?
Kerry: I get stuck doing the paper route with my brother on Saturdays. He aggravates me.

SCENARIO 3

Ted: What do you think of the new band instructor?
John: He makes me so embarrassed by having our section play alone.

SCENARIO 4

Kate: Why don't you ask the new girl to play tetherball with us?
Cindy: When she's around me, she makes me so shy I can't even say "Hi!"

SCENARIO 5

David: How did you do on the math test today?
Diane: Who knows! Ms. Kane makes me so nervous I can hardly add 2 + 2!

SCENARIO 6

Jesse: Are your parents sending you to camp this summer?
Mary: When you have to do chores every day to get one week of camp, it makes you pretty up-tight!

ROLE-PLAY SCRIPTS FOR "I FEEL...." SENTENCES
LEVEL II

SCENARIO 1

Karen: What's everyone doing after the game tonight?
Sarah: Chad makes me so mad! He's making me wait around until all of the players are out of the locker room.

SCENARIO 2

Jason: Want to study together this weekend?
Kerry: That Jean! I get stuck going to the library with her every Saturday. She aggravates me.

SCENARIO 3

Ted: What do you think of the new band instructor?
John: He makes me so embarrassed by having our section play alone.

SCENARIO 4

Kate: Why don't you ask him to the dance?
Cindy: When he's around me, he makes me so shy I can't even say "Hi!"

SCENARIO 5

David: How did you do on the math test today?
Diane: Who knows! Ms. Kane makes me so nervous I can hardly add 2 + 2!

SCENARIO 6

Jesse: Are your parents going to lend you the money for the ski trip?
Mary: When you have to baby-sit every weekend for a month to get one crummy ski trip, it makes you pretty up-tight!

Rephrase Feeling Statements

TRANSFER

OBJECTIVE

Group members will practice "I feel...." statements away from group by completing the **I Feel....?** sheet.

MATERIALS

I Feel...? sheet (Experience 5.4)

PROCEDURE

At the end of a group that has focused on making "I" statements, the facilitator directs members to complete the **I Feel...?** sheet for next time. On the sheet are examples of statements in which feelings aren't "owned" by the speaker. Group members rewrite them in the spaces provided, starting each re-write with "I feel....", "I felt...." or "I am feeling....".

I FEEL ....?

Restate each sentence so that speakers take responsibility for their own feelings.

1. My brother infuriates me. He steals from me.

   I feel _____

   when _____ .

2. All this emphasis on test scores bothers me!

   I feel _____

   about _____ .

3. Math is a frustrating subject.

   I _____

   _____ .

4. No one pays attention to me.

   I _____

   _____ .

5. Today was perfect. Everyone made me so happy.

   _____

   _____ .

6. Jake irritates me when he brags about his bike.

   _____

   _____ .

7. Thunder and lightning scare people.

   _____

   _____ .

8. Liver and onions makes me sick.

   _____

   _____ .

Heart Colors

AWARENESS

OBJECTIVE

Group members will draw multicolored heart pictures and label feelings for each color.

MATERIALS

Drawing paper, crayons or pens

PROCEDURE

The facilitator leads a discussion about how feelings are aften associated with the heart and with colors. For example, the heart shape is the symbol of love and affection. People are heard saying things like "My heart is full of sadness," "I'm heartbroken," and "I feel joy in my heart." The color red is frequently associated with anger, blue with sorrow, green with envy, and black with depression. Group members draw large heart shapes and make bands of different colors, following the outline of the heart shape. Members identify feeling words they associate with a given color and tell why, whenever possible. In this awareness-raising exercise, there are no right or wrong answers.

Feeling Color Wheel
PRACTICE

OBJECTIVE

Group members will associate feeling words with colors by completing a feeling color wheel.

MATERIALS

Feeling Color Wheel sheet (Experience 5.5), crayons, colored chalk or pencils

PROCEDURE

The facilitator passes out the Feeling Color Wheel and leads a discussion, reviewing common feeling/color associations. Two or three examples re discussed, with the remaining feeling words left for individual interpretation. Group members then color the wheels individually and come back to the group for discussion. There are no right or wrong answers.

If this is difficult for any group member, some suggested associations are:

red - anger	green - envy
blue - sadness/sorrow	black - depression
white - hope	purple - anxiety
pink - happiness/health	yellow - cheerfulness/thoughtfulness

Feeling Color Wheel

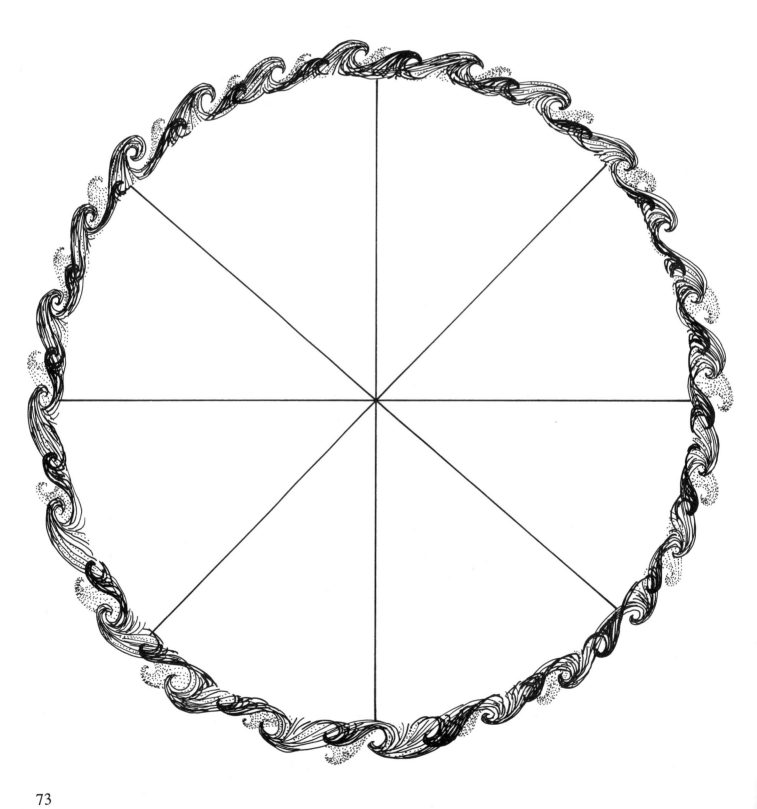

Painting Feelings
MORE PRACTICE

OBJECTIVE

Group members will paint abstract pictures to represent different feeling states.

MATERIALS

Paper, watercolors, Feelings Vocabulary sheet (Experience 5.1)

PROCEDURE

Group members are given paper and paints and then instructed to choose a feeling word from the list. Participants paint colors and abstract shapes they associate with a particular feeling. The pictures are shared with the group and members explain their choice of colors used to depict the chosen feeling.

Exploring Feelings
TRANSFER

OBJECTIVE

Group members will select a feeling they have had and complete a series of sentences and drawings about that feeling.

MATERIALS

Explore-a-Feeling sheet (Experience 5.6), pens

PROCEDURE

Each group member is given an Explore-a-Feeling sheet to complete at home and to bring for discussion at the beginning of the next group meeting.

As stated at the beginning of this chapter, being able to identify and express feelings is a foundation tool for each People Skill explored in *BELONGING*. Group members focus on feeling states at every People Skills meeting. Being clear about how group members are feeling is essential for an individual's success in the upcoming chapter, titled "Cooperating with Others."

EXPLORE-A-FEELING

DIRECTIONS: Select a feeling you sometimes have, such as anger, sadness, happiness, or joy. Complete the following information about that feeling.

PORTRAIT OF_____ FEELING_____.
                      Name

When I feel _____, I look like this:

I feel _____when_____

_____.

A color that goes with this feeling is:

(color the heart)

When I feel _____, I like to_____

_____.

The last time I felt _____was _____

_____.

Draw a picture of what happened on the back of this page or on a new sheet of paper.

FACILITATOR LOG

Things to remember:

_____

_____

_____

_____

_____

_____

_____

_____

_____

_____

_____

_____

_____

_____

_____

_____

_____

_____

_____

_____

_____

Cooperating
with Others

Chapter 6

Cooperating With Others

The group experiences many members are having through People Skills training represent their first successful attempts at belonging to a group. The series of activities under the heading "Cooperating with Others" is sequential in nature, taking participants from working together with one or two people to participating in increasingly larger groups. The intent is to demonstrate behaviors required to successfully integrate into a desired group and maintain a position of acceptance. Group members focus on feelings associated with being part of a unit. Some advantages of successful working, playing, and being together, i.e., cooperating with others are explored.

I. **PURPOSE** -- to encourage group members to risk connecting with one other person

Mirror Images
AWARENESS

OBJECTIVE

Group members will work together in pairs to create the "mirror image" of each other.

MATERIALS

Human resources only

PROCEDURE

Group members are divided into pairs. Initially, one person leads and the other imitates the leader's movements. Roles are then switched so each has a chance to lead and to follow. Eventually, no one leads and both partners contribute to the motion. Partners look each other in the eye and have slow, smooth, flowing motions. (Quick, abrupt movements are difficult to follow.) Once one set of partners practices mirroring each other, new partnerships are formed.

Suggestions for follow-up discussion:

1. Were you able to move together with your partner?
2. How did it feel when you both began to move as one?
3. Do you think you cooperated?

Cooperative Drawings
PRACTICE

OBJECTIVE

Group members will work cooperatively with one another to complete a drawing.

MATERIALS

Construction paper, crayons, colored pencils, felt pens

PROCEDURE

The facilitator explains to the group that each member will have a partner and jointly draw a picture. Group members either choose a partner or are randomly assigned one. The dynamics of the experience are frequently very different, depending upon whether or not members choose to work together. All persons have an opportunity to draw something on their own sides of the paper. The dyad then draws something together in the middle of the page. The center drawing is something mutually agreed upon and drawn (see diagram suggestions). Members are encouraged to have a planning discussion **before** drawing. Both people are in agreement **before** beginning the product.

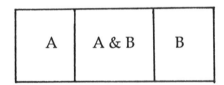   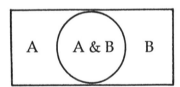

Follow-up discussion:

1. Is it easy for you to share your "space" with someone?
2. How do you feel about your final product?
3. Are there advantages to working together with someone else?
4. Do you think you and your partner cooperated? What does that mean to you? What did you do that showed "cooperation"?

Suggestion: The facilitator lists all of the behaviors noted as examples of cooperation. This list is posted to help group members evaluate future cooperative experiences.

Silent Drawings

MORE PRACTICE

OBJECTIVE

Group members will work cooperatively with one another to complete a drawing.

MATERIALS

Construction paper, crayons, felt pens

PROCEDURE

The facilitator explains that the activity is a cooperative drawing done without any talking. Members choose their partners or are randomly paired by the facilitator. The facilitator explains that members will share a piece of paper. Members select their own colored felt pen or crayon. Partners complete a cooperative picture without talking. They may use hand signals, facial expressions, or other body language to communicate about their product.

Suggestion for follow-up discussion:

1. How did you feel about this cooperative drawing compared to the one done previously?
2. How did you feel when you wanted to talk to your partner and couldn't?
3. Did you enjoy this activity? Why or why not?
4. How did you feel about your finished drawing?
5. Did you work equally on the drawing?

Cooperative Collage
STILL MORE PRACTICE

OBJECTIVE

Group members will demonstrate the ability to take turns with one other person to complete a project.

MATERIALS

Construction paper, crayons, colored pencils, felt pens. For variations: finger paints; paper; clay/Playdough; an assortment of construction items, such as pipe cleaners, glue, glitter, magazine pictures, buttons, sticks

PROCEDURE

Members select partners or are randomly assigned one. The partners agree on a single drawing project to be created by both. One person draws or makes the first part of the project, working for about two minutes. The next person adds to the creation and returns it to the first person to add on another part, and so on.

The exercise is varied by using finger paints to create a single picture while taking turns. Sculptures made out of Playdough or clay are achieved with the same "taking turns" format. Creative collages using the assorted materials listed above are made by members using the cooperative "add-on" system.

In a follow-up discussion, group members respond to some of the following questions:

1. How do you feel about your finished product?
2. How did you feel during this experience?
3. How did you decide what to make?
4. What were the advantages and disadvantages of creating something with another person?
5. Did you trust your partner when it was that person's turn to add on to the project?

Cooperative Survey

TRANSFER

OBJECTIVE

Group members will interact with someone of their choice to complete a cooperative survey.

MATERIALS

Cooperative Survey (Experience 6.1)

PROCEDURE

The leader gives each group member a Cooperative Survey. The sheet is to be worked on away from the group with a chosen family member or friend and then brought to the next meeting. Members begin the next meeting with a sharing of surveys. As a follow-up, members get together in pairs and do the Cooperative Survey within the group. The activity can be repeated periodically with changes in survey sheet information.

COOPERATIVE SURVEY

1. My name is

_____

Today's date is

_____

2. The person who worked on this with me is

_____.

3. I enjoy _____, and

my partner enjoys _____.

4. We both remember when _____.

5. One of my strengths is _____, and

my partner's strength is _____.

6. One of my weaknesses is _____, and

my partner's weakness is _____.

7. A hobby I have is _____, and

a hobby my partner has is _____.

8. We each have a favorite place. Mine is _____,

and my partner's favorite is _____.

9. In my spare time, I _____,

and my partner _____.

10. When I feel lonely, I _____,

and my partner _____.

II. PURPOSE -- to encourage members to participate in group experiences involving two to four other people

People Machines
AWARENESS

OBJECTIVE

Members will cooperatively participate to pantomime a machine.

MATERIALS

Human resources only

PROCEDURE

Members are divided into groups of two to four. The facilitator explains that each group will create its own machine. The idea is demonstrated first by three volunteers. The facilitator explains that they will create a washing machine. Two people hold hands with outstretched arms. The third person is between the others, moving around as the "laundry." Other possibilities include a dishwasher, car, typewriter, or computer.

Members are given several minutes to create one of the above-mentioned machines or one of their own choice. Machines are demonstrated to the rest of the group. Members try to guess what the machine is.

An extension of this activity happens when groups create "imaginary machines" with sounds and motions. Groups take time to build and rehearse their "machines" before demonstrating them to the large group.

Suggestions for follow-up discussion:

1. Did everyone in your group participate?
2. Did anyone in your group tell others what to do? If so, how did it feel to be told what part you had to play?
3. Did you enjoy demonstrating your machine to others? Why or why not?

Group Puzzle Pictures
PRACTICE

OBJECTIVE

Group members will work together in groups of three or four to build a puzzle, design a picture, and complete the picture.

MATERIALS

Large, white construction paper cut into five or six odd-shaped pieces; crayons; colored pens or pencils; tape

PROCEDURE

Groups of three or four are formed either by self-selection (who would like to work with whom) or random selection (putting names in a hat and drawing out three or four). Each group is given a set of puzzle pieces which when taped together form an 11" X 18" sheet of white construction paper. It is helpful for the facilitator to mark the back of each puzzle piece to assist group members when assembling the pieces. Group members work together to tape the pieces on the back side. Next, members decide on a theme for the picture, and each member contributes by drawing a part of the picture. While this process is unfolding, the facilitator helps mediate conflicts and makes suggestions if groups "get stuck." The leader also keeps a list of cooperative behaviors observed. In a follow-up discussion, group members share their products and identify cooperative and uncooperative experiences they had in their groups. The facilitator lists these for future reference.

Coming To Consensus
MORE PRACTICE

OBJECTIVE

Groups of three or four people will make consensual decisions about things everyone likes and dislikes.

MATERIALS

Consensus Sheet (Experience 6.2), pencils

PROCEDURE

Groups of three or four are formed either by self or random selection. Each group is given a Consensus Sheet and is directed to select a recorder consensually, not by "majority rules." The facilitator guides the group through the process of selecting a recorder by suggesting that:

1. one person submits a name.
2. each person takes 30 seconds to say whether they agree or disagree with the selection.
3. if most people agree but one or two firmly disagree, then another name is submitted.
4. if one or more people continually block choices, the group talks about their reasons for always blocking and the possibility for compromise.
5. if one or more people continually shift positions to go with the opinion of the majority, the group talks about reasons for always giving in and the possible group benefits of holding firm when feeling strongly about an issue.

When a recorder has been selected, each group is given a Consensus Sheet and begins the process of discovering personal likes and dislikes which everyone has in common (Experience 6.2). The process outlined previously is utilized again, with a recorder monitoring equal time for each member. The recorder also writes down agreed-upon items on the Consensus Sheet.

In a follow-up discussion, members talk about experiences they had in the consensus group, such as:

1. What was the hardest part about coming to a consensus?
2. How did it feel to use a consensus rather than "majority rules" method?
3. How was everyone guaranteed the opportunity to join in the process?
4. How did it feel to compromise? To block?
5. How can consensus be used in other situations? At other times in this group?

CONSENSUS SHEET

	LIKES	DISLIKES
T V SHOW		
SPORT		
FRUIT		
DESSERT		
MUSIC GROUP		

Odds And Ends Creations
STILL MORE PRACTICE

OBJECTIVE

Group members will use an assortment of items to create a cooperative sculpture.

MATERIALS

Paper scraps, cans, pipe cleaners, Popsicle sticks, glue, glitter, scissors, buttons, boxes, cardboard tubes, egg cartons, other small items

PROCEDURE

Groups of three or four are formed by self or random selection. Each group is given a similar set of odds and ends and is instructed to work together to create a single sculpture. The facilitator may give a name to the creations the groups are making, for example: "Clunko," a "Tiptover," a "Ginjac." Members can make whatever they want their creations to be. They are asked to talk about it before starting. Everyone adds to the final creation.

In a follow-up discussion group members respond to questions, such as:

1. How did your group cooperate? Give examples of cooperative behavior.
2. Was this easy or hard to do?
3. Tell about your "Clunko." What does it do? Where does it live? How is it feeling and why?
4. How did your group decide what to make? Was it a consensual decision?
5. What was your part in the project?
6. How do you like participating in a group effort?

Variation: Groups are given only paper strips and one large sheet of construction paper, one pair of scissors, and one bottle of glue. Groups build 3-D sculptures by rolling, folding, and twisting paper strips and gluing them to the large sheet of paper. Discussions about what to make and who does what are encouraged by the facilitator, who also makes note of demonstrated cooperative behaviors for follow-up discussion.

Journal Writing - Cooperating At Home

TRANSFER

OBJECTIVE

Members will write in their journals about ways they cooperate at home with their families.

MATERIALS

Journals, pencils or pens

PROCEDURE

Through discussion, the group brainstorms to create a list of chores and ways that they are helpful and cooperative at home. Using the following suggestions as a guide, group members write about one or more of the following family activities discussed as it relates to them:

1. cleaning the house
2. preparing meals
3. helping with younger siblings
4. getting ready for a trip/vacation
5. resolving a conflict

III. **PURPOSE** -- to encourage members to actively participate in groups with more than four people

Knot Game
AWARENESS

OBJECTIVE

Group members will cooperate to create and then untangle a "knot" of people.

MATERIALS

An open space

PROCEDURE

Group members, holding hands, form a large circle. One member is chosen to leave the room while the remaining members tangle themselves. They can twist, turn, step over others, or make other movements, as long as they continue to hold hands. Once this knot of people is formed, the chosen member returns to the group to untangle the knot. The person selected directs the others in an attempt to untangle the members. In the beginning, the members are silent while the one person is working. The person may ask for suggestions if help is needed. The game is over when all are in the full circle once again.

Suggestions for follow-up discussion:

1. Did you feel everyone worked together to untangle the knot?
2. How did it feel when you were still tangled and others weren't?
3. Did you enjoy this activity?

Five Squares - Six-Inch Puzzle

PRACTICE

OBJECTIVE

Each member will participate with a group to form five six-inch squares from puzzle pieces.

MATERIALS

Five Squares - Six-Inch Puzzle sheet (Experience 6.3), previously cut into pieces by the facilitator

PROCEDURE

This activity requires group cooperation in order for it to be successful. The facilitator carefully explains the activity directions as noted on Experience 6.3 before passing out the pieces. Each group then works to complete five six-inch squares.

Suggestions for follow-up discussion:

1. How did it feel to be part of a team effort?
2. What did various team members do to demonstrate cooperation?
3. In general, did your group cooperate?

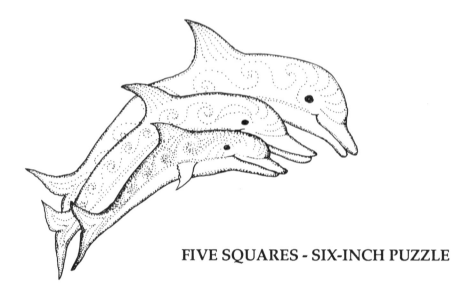

FIVE SQUARES - SIX-INCH PUZZLE

DIRECTIONS FOR MAKING:

Cut tagboard or other substantial material according to patterns given and mark each with the appropriate letter. All measurement is precise so that pieces interchange accurately. Place all of the A's, B's, C's, D's, and E's needed to complete the five six-inch puzzles in an envelope. Have the same number of envelopes as there are groups doing the activity.

PROCEDURE:

Groups of five people sit around a table or other hard surface. Each group is given an envelope with puzzle pieces. Each player within a group takes the pieces marked with a different letter of the alphabet.

GOAL:

To have each player form one six-inch square.

GROUND RULES:

1. You may pass your pieces to other players, if you see they need them.
2. You may **not** talk.
3. You may **not** gesture.
4. You may **not** touch someone else's puzzle piece unless that person gives you one.

FIVE SQUARES - SIX-INCH PUZZLE PATTERNS

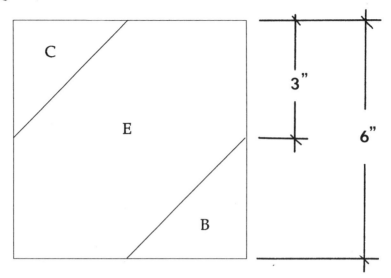

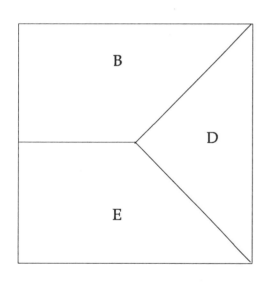

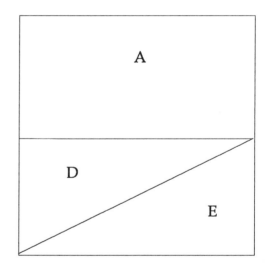

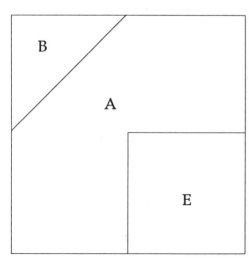

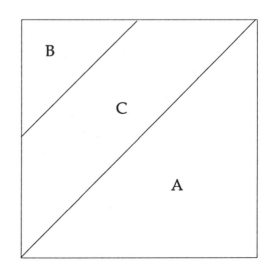

Assembly Line

MORE PRACTICE

OBJECTIVE

Groups will work with other groups in an assembly line to complete a project, such as greeting cards.

MATERIALS

Colored construction paper, felt pens, scissors, glue, other items for making a group project

PROCEDURE

The facilitator explains that the group is going to work together to form an assembly line. The end product will be greeting cards. The concept of assembly line is pursued. The facilitator emphasizes that each person has a specific job and that it is important to do that job well and as quickly as possible. The group discusses the importance of cooperation in getting a job done. Members sit in groups as if on a real industrial assembly line with a conveyor belt.

Suggested jobs (some members may need to do more than one job):

1. cutter/folder - cuts paper to desired size and folds it
2. verse writer - writes greeting card verse
3. printer - prints the greeting and the price on the card
4. front-page illustrator - draws/decorates front of card to go with the greeting or verse
5. envelope maker - creates the holder for the card

Suggested topics for follow-up discussion:

1. Did everyone work together, cooperate?
2. What happened when someone didn't cooperate?
3. Did you get bored with your job?
4. What happened when someone didn't pay attention?
5. How do you feel about the finished product?

Groups And Me
TRANSFER

OBJECTIVE

Group members tell how they feel while participating in different group situations.

MATERIALS

Groups and Me sheet (Experience 6.4)

PROCEDURE

The facilitator asks group members to complete the Groups and Me sheet to bring to the next session. Time is taken at the next meeting to review these responses.

Throughout the cooperation experiences, group members are encouraged to consider their own needs in relation to the needs of others. In the next chapter, "Asserting Yourself," group members explore behaviors which are developed to assure that one's individual perspective is clearly recognized within the group context and that one's unique contributions are heard by others.

GROUPS AND ME

Choose a word to complete each sentence. You may use the words listed below or make up your own.

important	generous	honest
entertaining	helpful	fair
friendly	kind	loyal

1. When I am part of a group, I feel _____.

2. I enjoy working in any _____

   group because _____.

3. On my first day at this school, everyone seemed very _____

   and I felt _____.

4. When I am asked to join a group, I feel _____.

5. Groups like me because I am _____.

6. I felt_____when the group excluded me because

   _____.

7. I like working in groups because _____

   _____.

8. When I'm with my friends, I feel _____.

9. Groups I have belonged to are_____

   _____.

10. Describe a time when you felt you really contributed something to a group.

    Explain how you felt_____

    _____

    _____

FACILITATOR LOG

Things to remember:

_____

_____

_____

_____

_____

_____

_____

_____

_____

_____

_____

_____

_____

_____

_____

_____

_____

_____

_____

Asserting
Yourself

Chapter 7

Asserting Yourself

Assertive skills development is included as a component of People Skills training. Practicing and mastering simple assertive tools reinforces feelings of self-worth as discussed in the "Exploring Self" chapter. Facility with assertive techniques allows for the possibility of greater success in the cooperative endeavors outlined in "Cooperating with Others" chapter. Assertive behavior is necessary for successfully resolving conflicts and for having comfortable conversations, which are the focuses of upcoming sections.

Many books and extensive training programs are available for teaching/learning assertive skills. The training here is basic and involves three levels. First, group members learn to identify passive, aggressive, and assertive behaviors on the basis of body language and the content of a statement. Next, participants practice making assertive statements, refusals, and requests. Finally, more complex interactions are explored, with members learning assertive tools for diffusing "power plays."

I. **PURPOSE** -- to assist group members in identifying passive, aggressive, and assertive behaviors

Identifying Behaviors
AWARENESS

OBJECTIVE

Group members will identify passive, aggressive, and assertive behaviors.

MATERIALS

People or puppets

PROCEDURE

The facilitator explains the characteristics of passive, aggressive, and assertive behaviors as stated below:

Passive - People who demonstrate passive behaviors:

1. often say "yes" when they want to say "no"
2. seem afraid to share real feelings or thoughts
3. have little or no eye contact with others
4. speak softly and infrequently
5. often slouch and shrug their shoulders

Aggressive - People who behave aggressively:

1. make statements without consideration for the feelings of others
2. often appear to be angry when really feeling hurt, embarrassed, sad, left out, frustrated, inadequate, or other emotion
3. frequently abuse others physically and/or verbally
4. behave in a manner that is loud, threatening, insulting, and/or manipulative

Assertive - People who demonstrate assertive behaviors:

1. are honest and direct
2. choose to tell others what they like or dislike, want or don't want
3. speak in a calm, firm voice
4. look at others while speaking
5. accept responsibility for the choices they make

The facilitator models these behaviors. For example, when discussing a passive person, facilitator speaks in a quiet voice, slouches, shuffles feet, or uses other appropriate body language. Group members are asked to demonstrate these behaviors also. Puppets are effective tools for introducing these behaviors to young children.

Which Is It -- Passive, Aggressive Or Assertive?

PRACTICE

OBJECTIVE

Group members will label responses as passive, aggressive, or assertive.

MATERIALS

Passive, Aggressive, Assertive sheet (Experiences 7.1, 7.2), pencils

PROCEDURE

Group members are given copies of either Experience 7.1 or 7.2. Members complete sheets in pairs or triads so discussion is encouraged. The facilitator asks members to consider:

1. How do I usually deal with similar situations?
2. How do I feel when I handle situations in this way?
3. How do I feel just being in this situation?
4. What are some alternate assertive responses?
5. What are possible consequences for behaving passively, aggressively, or assertively in each case?

Personal insights gained in the small-group experience are shared by members with the entire group. The facilitator asks all members to consider: "What is the 'payoff' that keeps you handling situations in the same manner?" "What do you 'get' by being either consistently passive, aggressive, or assertive?"

PASSIVE, AGGRESSIVE, OR ASSERTIVE?
LEVEL I

For the following situations, mark each response as:

AG = aggressive   AS = assertive   P = passive

Situation 1

Your teacher made a mistake correcting your spelling test.

Response:

_____ "Hey! You didn't do this right."
_____ Do nothing.
_____ "I think this word is spelled correctly. Would you check it again?"

Situation 2

You get the wrong change from a store clerk.

Response:

_____ Walk away and say nothing.
_____ "What are you trying to do-cheat me or something?"
_____ "Excuse me, I believe you gave me the wrong change."

Situation 3

Imagine a friend of yours asked to copy your homework.

Response:

_____ "No! That's cheating!"
_____ "I really spent a lot of time on this assignment. I don't want to let you copy my work."
_____ "I guess so."

Situation 4

You're playing a team game and some people on your team aren't participating.

Response:

_____ Say nothing.
_____ "If you're not going to play the game, get lost!"
_____ "I noticed you didn't participate with the team. Was something wrong?"

Situation 5

Someone asks you to go somewhere and you really don't want to go.

Response:

_____ "Are you kidding?"
_____ "Thanks for asking, and I'd rather not."
_____ "I don't think I can."

Situation 6

Your parents haven't talked to you about the notice you brought home from school about sign-ups for soccer. You really want to join the team.

Response:

_____ "Big help they are! They don't care if I have fun."
_____ Say nothing and hope someone brings it up.
_____ "I'd really like to play soccer. Here's information about signing up for the team."

Situation 7

You've just been offered some ice cream and you're allergic to milk.

Response:

_____ "No, thanks."
_____ "Well, I guess I could have a little."
_____ "You've got to be kidding! That stuff makes me sick!"

PASSIVE, AGGRESSIVE, OR ASSERTIVE?
LEVEL II

For the following situations, mark each response as:

AG = aggressive   AS = assertive   P = passive

Situation 1

A teacher has made a mistake grading an exam.

Response:

_____ "You cheated me out of 10 points on this test!"
_____ Do nothing.
_____ "I've discovered an error in the way this exam was graded."

Situation 2

You get the wrong change from a store clerk.

Response:

_____ Walk away and say nothing.
_____ "What are you trying to do-cheat me or something?"
_____ "Excuse me, I believe you gave me the incorrect amount of money back."

Situation 3

Imagine a friend of yours asks to copy your homework.

Response:

_____ "No! That's cheating!"
_____ "I spent a lot of time on this assignment. I am unwilling to let you copy my work."
_____ "I guess so."

Situation 4

You're doing a group project and not all of the group members are doing their share of the work.

Response:

_____ Say nothing.
_____ "If you're not going to help with the project, just get out of here!"
_____ "I noticed that you haven't helped on our project. Is something wrong?"

Situation 5

Someone asks you to go somewhere and you really don't want to go.

Response:

_____ "Are you kidding?"
_____ "I appreciate the invitation, and I'd rather not."
_____ "I don't think I can."

Situation 6

You've been offered several jobs and want help deciding among them. No one has offered an opinion.

Response:

_____ "Big help they are! They don't care if I get the best job or not. They don't care about me."
_____ Say nothing and hope someone offers advice.
_____ "I've been giving this a lot of thought and need someone to help me. Are you willing to listen?"

Situation 7

You've just been offered alcohol at a party and you don't drink.

Response:

_____ "No, thank you."
_____ "Well, I guess I could have a little drink."
_____ "You've got to be kidding! Don't you know what that stuff does to your body!"

Journal Writing - Assertive Behaviors

TRANSFER

OBJECTIVE

Group members will identify assertive behaviors in daily living situations and write examples in journals.

MATERIALS

Journal

PROCEDURE

Group members are asked to pay close attention on a daily basis to interactions they have or others around them have. Each is asked to record any examples of assertive behavior noticed and to describe what made it seem assertive. Examples of passive or aggressive exchanges are noted as well, if desired. The primary aim is to assist members in becoming attuned to-and increasingly more comfortable with-assertive behaviors.

II. **PURPOSE** -- to help group members "stand up for themselves" and make assertive requests and refusals

Analyzing Requests, Refusals, And Responses
AWARENESS

OBJECTIVE

Group members will discuss the effectiveness of different ways of responding, requesting, and refusing.

MATERIALS

Assertive Analysis (Experience 7.3)

PROCEDURE

The facilitator asks group members to read each example in Experience 7.3. After each one, members are asked to consider such questions as:

1. Does this give a clear message to the receiver?
2. What is the speaker "really" saying?
3. What might your response be if someone said this to you?
4. What would your expectations be if someone said this to you? How would you feel?
5. Is this an assertive statement? If not, how can it be changed to be one?

ASSERTIVE ANALYSIS

REQUESTS

1. That cake really looks delicious. I bet it tastes good, too.

2. I need a piece of that cake. Give me a big one!

3. I'd really like a piece of cake. May I have some?

4. I don't suppose there's any extra cake?

5. If there's any cake left over, I'd like a piece.

6. Hi! I wonder if you'd consider sharing your cake with me?

REFUSALS

1. Don't be ridiculous! Of course, I don't want to run with you!

2. I don't think running is good for my knees.

3. I need new jogging shoes.

4. No, I don't want to run today.

5. No, I don't run because running hurts my knees. I like to swim. We could do that together.

6. Gee, I'm not sure about that.

RESPONSES

Statement: I don't think you are cut out for that job.
Response: I really don't care what you think!

Statement: I wonder if that job's for you.
Response: I've thought about it a lot. I'm going to try it for these reasons.

Statement: Have you really considered this job and all the work it involves?
Response: Gosh, I don't know about that.

Statement: Are you positive about taking this job?
Response: I feel there's some risk involved, and I'm prepared to accept that fact.

Practicing Assertive Refusals

PRACTICE

OBJECTIVE

Group members will make assertive refusals in role-play situations.

MATERIALS

Role-Play Situation Cards - Assertive Refusals (Experiences 7.4, 7.5) Cards are cut apart by the facilitator prior to the group meeting.

PROCEDURE

The facilitator reviews ways to make assertive refusals by modeling the following refusals:

> "No, thank you."
> "No, I don't want to do that."
> "No, I'd rather not."
> "No, and thanks for asking."
> "No, that's not something I want to do."
> "No, I need to be alone now."
> "No, I don't feel comfortable doing that."

The facilitator leads a discussion, explaining that all people have the right to not want to do things that others want them to do. The facilitator then opens the discussion to group members to talk about situations in which it is appropriate to make an assertive refusal. The facilitator asks group members to consider possible consequences when using assertive refusals both (1) with parents or others in authority and when (2) the request refutes a responsibility or an agreement previously made.

Members use the Role-Play Situation Cards, Level I or II, (Experience 7.4 or 7.5) to practice making assertive refusals.

ROLE-PLAY SITUATION CARDS - ASSERTIVE REFUSALS
LEVEL I

A teacher accuses you of cheating on a test. You know you didn't.

You say:

Your dad wants you to join the soccer team. You aren't interested in joining.

You say:

You are in a store and a friend asks you to help steal.

You say:

Your best friend invites you to go to the movies. You are on restriction and know your parents won't let you go.

You say:

A friend asks you to play at recess. You don't want to play.

You say:

A stranger offers you a ride home. You feel uncomfortable.

You say:

A neighbor who is going on vacation asks you to feed the pets. Your family already has something planned. You won't be able to do this.

You say:

A friend asks you to go bike riding. Your parents aren't home. You have to have their permission before you can go.

You say:

A friend asks to copy your homework. You worked hard on yours.

You say:

A friend asks to look at some answers on your test.

You say:

ROLE-PLAY SITUATION CARDS - ASSERTIVE REFUSALS
LEVEL II

An instructor accuses you of cheating on a test.

You say:

A friend asks to look at your answers on a test.

You say:

You are in a store. A friend asks you to steal something.

You say:

A friend offers you a ride in his dad's car. You know he doesn't have a driver's license.

You say:

You are asked out by someone you don't want to date.

You say:

Your best friend offers you a ticket to a great rock concert. You'd love to go. Your parents require chaperones.

You say:

A neighbor asks if you can baby-sit Friday night, but you already have plans.

You say:

Your dad was on his high school football team. He wants you to sign up, and you're not interested.

You say:

You are at a party and a friend offers you drugs.

You say:

A friend asks you to cut class together.

You say:

Practicing Assertive Requests
MORE PRACTICE

OBJECTIVE

Group members will make requests assertively.

MATERIALS

Role-Play Situation Cards - Assertive Requests (Experiences 7.6, 7.7)

PROCEDURE

The facilitator defines "making a request" as asking for something desired. In addition, the facilitator explains that making assertive requests is asking for something in a way that considers the feelings of others. When making an assertive request, one needs to

1. look at the person
2. be honest and direct
3. speak in a calm, firm voice
4. begin by using "I" statements, such as
   "I want...." and "I need...."

The facilitator emphasizes that even though people ask for something, they may not always get what is requested. And yet, if they don't ask, they stand less chance of reaching the desired end.

Before passing out the Role-Play Situation Cards, the facilitator models several role-play examples and uses appropriate tone of voice and body language.

ROLE-PLAY SITUATION CARDS - ASSERTIVE REQUESTS
LEVEL I

You are buying something at a store. The salesclerk gives you the incorrect amount of change.

You say:

You forget your homework assignment at your house. You need to tell your teacher.

You say:

You see a group of kids playing together. You'd like to join them.

You say:

Several of your friends are going to a movie together. They haven't invited you and you want to join them.

You say:

A friend borrowed one of your toys and hasn't returned it. You'd like it back.

You say:

You feel your parents should increase your allowance.

You say:

You are lost at an amusement park and go to a ticket booth for help.

You say:

You don't understand how to do some math problems. You want your teacher to explain it again.

You say:

You asked your mom a week ago if you could go to summer camp. She hasn't given you an answer and you'd like to know.

You say:

A friend borrowed some money from you, and hasn't returned it. You need it to buy something.

You say:

ROLE-PLAY SITUATION CARDS - ASSERTIVE REQUESTS
LEVEL II

You buy a new pair of pants and discover they are ripped when you get them home. You take them back to the salesclerk.

You say:

You want to join a group of friends who are playing ball.

You say:

A friend has been teasing you about your new haircut.

You say:

You are with several friends who are going to a movie. They haven't invited you and you want to join them.

You say:

You are standing in line to buy tickets and someone cuts in front of you.

You say:

You are taking a math class and don't understand a new concept. You would like your teacher to explain it again.

You say:

You are in a department store and need to find a restroom.

You say:

You audition for a play and want to participate. The director turns you down.

You say:

A friend borrowed $10 from you and hasn't returned it.

You say:

You are at a restaurant and haven't been waited on yet. After fifteen minutes you decide to go talk to the head waiter.

You say:

"Please" And "No, Thank You"

TRANSFER

OBJECTIVE

Group members will write assertive requests and refusals.

MATERIALS

Assertive Requests and Refusals (Experience 7.8)

PROCEDURE

Group members are given copies of Experience 7.8. Members complete worksheets by writing both an assertive request and a refusal to each of the following individuals: self, Mom/Dad, friend, teacher/leader. The facilitator suggests that members use one of the sample request and refusal statements at the bottom of the exercise or create one of their own. Group members share their requests and refusals with each other. The facilitator encourages members to share what they've written and then practiced with the person to whom the request/refusal was directed.

ASSERTIVE REQUESTS AND REFUSALS

SELF	MOM/DAD
Request -	Request -
Refusal -	Refusal -
FRIEND	**TEACHER/LEADER**
Request -	Request -
Refusal -	Refusal -

SAMPLES

REQUESTS

_____(name)_____ , I need _____.

_____(name)_____ , I want _____.

_____(name)_____ , I'd like _____.

REFUSALS

No, _____(name)_____ , I don't want to _____.

_____(name)_____ , I don't feet comfortable doing _____.

_____(name)_____ , I'd rather not _____ , but thanks for asking.

III. **PURPOSE** -- to improve assertive skills in order to diffuse "power plays"

Power Plays
AWARENESS

OBJECTIVE

Group members will recognize "power plays" when examples are given.

MATERIALS

Power Plays sheets (Experiences 7.9, 7.10)

PROCEDURE

The facilitator leads group members through a discussion of the occurrence of power plays in daily living. Power plays are presented as human interactions in which there is a "one-up" and "one-down" position and in which someone "wins" and someone "loses." Strong emotions accompany power plays. The discussion includes an emphasis on the fact that learning to diffuse power plays and developing cooperative skills for resolving conflicts on an individual level promote peace in a much broader realm: peace on earth. Group members read through the power plays samples in Experience 7.9 or 7.10, noting the one-up/one-down and win/lose qualities of each. They also identify probable feelings which would accompany the scenarios.

POWER PLAYS
LEVEL I

SCENE I

Person #1:   Let's play ball this afternoon.
Person #2:   I told Jeff I'd go skating.
Person #1:   Fine! Go ahead and do what he says all the time. I hate skating.
Person #2:   We went skating last week. I thought you had fun. Come join us!
Person #1:   I bet you weren't even going to ask me! Listen, forget about skating today or forget our friendship!

SCENE II

Person #1:   Jessie, you need a new pair of shoes. Those don't match your clothes.
Person #2:   Gosh, I kind of like them.
Person #1:   Look, they go better with my shorts than with yours. Tell you what-I'll give you my shoes and take those off your hands.
Person #2:   My shoes are pretty new.
Person #1:   Are you saying mine aren't? Hey, if you think I'm trying to cheat you, just say so! I was just trying to help you out!
Person #2:   Gee, thanks for helping me. I guess I don't match things too well, but I sure do like my new shoes.

Consider these questions for each scene:

1. Who had the "one-up" and "one-down" position in each scene?
2. Who was winner/loser?
3. How do you think each person was feeling?
4. How could being assertive have helped end these "power plays?"

128

POWER PLAYS
LEVEL II

SCENE I

Person #1: I need to talk with you. You need to get straight about my conversation with Jan.

Person #2: I don't need to "get straight" about anything! But I'll tell you a thing or two.

Person #1: What on earth could you, who "knows-it-all," tell me?

Person #2: I could tell you that you are constantly poking around in my business!

Person #1: (in tears) If you must know, it's just because I care about you!

SCENE II

Person #1: I made reservations for a ski weekend for us!

Person #2: Gosh, I'm not sure I want to do that.

Person #1: You'll love it! You can take lessons while I head for the mountaintops!

Person #2: Gee, I don't have warm enough clothes or boots or anything.

Person #1: The trouble with you is you're so afraid to try new things. You absolutely need this adventure!

Person #2: I guess I could try it out. I'd prefer a quiet weekend at home.

Person #1: Good heavens! How dull! Lighten up already!

Person #2: (halfheartedly) You're probably right. When are we going?

Consider these questions for each scene:

1. Who is winner/loser?
2. How is "one-up"/"one-down" demonstrated?
3. What are some possible feelings being experienced in each situation?
4. Are passive and aggressive behaviors represented in the dialogues?

Assertive Techniques

MORE AWARENESS

OBJECTIVE

Group members will identify and practice the assertive techniques of (1) broken record, (2) paraphrasing, and (3) negative inquiry.

MATERIALS

Assertive Skills (Experience 7.11)

PROCEDURE

Group members join in a discussion of three assertive techniques which are defined on the accompanying exercise sheet (Experience 7.11). Members are asked to apply the techniques to the two power plays presented in the previous awareness exercise. This can be accomplished by talking about how each could be used to change the course of the dialogue. Another means of practicing the skills requires group members to role play the people in the scenes and use assertive techniques to diffuse the power plays. Members are then asked to explain situations from their own lives in which the three techniques would have been helpful.

THREE ASSERTIVE TECHNIQUES:
BROKEN RECORD, NEGATIVE INQUIRY, PARAPHRASING

BROKEN RECORD is demonstrated by repeating what another person has said and consistently asserting your position. This technique is **not** effective in emotionally volatile situations. It tends to accelerate the intensity of emotion.

EXAMPLE:

#1: "I want to go roller-skating tonight."

#2: "I understand that you want to go roller-skating tonight, and I don't have any way to get you there."

#1: "But everyone is going tonight. I have to go."

#2: "I understand that you want to go roller-skating with everyone tonight, and I don't have any way to get you there."

#1: "Why can't you buy a new car. It's not fair!"

#2: "I understand that you think it's unfair to miss roller-skating, and I have no way of getting you there."

NEGATIVE INQUIRY is demonstrated by actively encouraging criticism to gain information or exhaust manipulations.

EXAMPLE:

#1: You really bugged me when you went hiking with Charlie.

#2: Really? What exactly was it that bothered you?

#1: You didn't ask me to go along.

#2: I don't quite understand. Tell me more, will you?

#1: You don't seem to want to do things with me anymore.

#2: How do you feel about that?

#1: Upset, left out, hurt.

#2: What would help?

PARAPHRASING occurs when someone's message restated by you demonstrates that the person was heard.

EXAMPLE:

#1: I was wondering why you volunteered to chair the panel discussion. You know I have done that for the past few years. Everyone says I do a great job. No one else has ever offered. I've always been asked in the past. Now you go and say you'll do it. I'm left out.

#2: You're wondering why I volunteered for a position you've done such a good job with for several years. I understand that you feel badly about my chairing the panel this year.

Role Playing Assertive Techniques

PRACTICE

OBJECTIVE

Group members will be able to apply three assertive techniques (broken record, negative inquiry and paraphrasing) to real-life situations.

MATERIALS

Assertive Role-Play Dialogues (Experience 7.12), chalkboard or paper, chalk or marker

PROCEDURE

Group members read the role play dialogues presented in Experience 7.12. Pairs volunteer to act out each scene as written and then attempt to utilize asssertive strategies to alter the scenario and diffuse the "power play."

Next, group members are asked to describe real-life power plays each has experienced. The dialogue is written out and then role played by two volunteers. The two attempt to redirect the original scene by using one of the three assertive techniques studied.

ASSERTIVE ROLE-PLAY DIALOGUES

SCENE I

#1:   Go get my books for me.
#2:   Get your own books. You sure are lazy.
#1:   Knock off the name-calling! I happen to be really tired.
      A real friend would just go get the books!
#2:   Looks like I'm just not a real friend then! (stomps off)

SCENE II

#1:   If you want me to do my homework, then buy me that album
      I want.
#2:   Okay, Honey. I'll get it for you tomorrow.
#1:   No way! Go out and get it now, and then I'll hit the books.
#2:   Now, Honey, please be reasonable. The stores are closed.

SCENE III

#1:   I'm going to lose this sale if you don't get an earlier delivery date.
#2:   Everyone needs fast delivery.
#1:   This sale is bigger than anyone else's. You get me an earlier date!
#2:   Take a hike!
#1:   I can complain to the home office and don't think I won't!

SCENE IV

#1:   I want you home in the daytime. No job!
#2:   I'll do as I please!
#1:   Things are going to fall apart around here if you work.
#2:   Nonsense!
#1:   No job!
#2:   Want to bet?

Consensual Decisions

MORE PRACTICE

OBJECTIVE

Group members will experience cooperative decision-making to arrive at a consensus.

MATERIALS

$1 or less from each group member, chalkboard or chart paper, chalk or marker

PROCEDURE

Group members are asked to pool their contribution of $1 or less. The facilitator poses the question: "What shall we do with our fund?" Group members brainstorm possibilities, which are recorded on chart paper or a chalkboard. Next, each item is highlighted and members are polled as to whether they agree or disagree on whether to spend money for that item. Members also indicate whether they want to speak to an issue or not. The situation sounds as follows:

Item: We can use our fund to buy snacks for break time.

Member #1:   I agree.
Member #2:   I agree and want to speak to this choice.
Member #3:   I disagree.
Member #4:   I agree.
Member #5:   I disagree and want to speak to this choice.

Those who request to speak to a given item do so in an attempt to move for a consensus in favor of their position. Each item is handled in this manner until a consensus is reached as to which choices are eliminated and what the final choice is.

Consensual-decision making is expanded here from its simplified form in the section titled "Cooperating with Others." The purpose is to demonstrate to group members that it is possible to make decisions and to interact with others from positions of equal power, i.e., without the win/lose of a power play. Members are asked to consider and discuss the benefits of cooperative behavior. Some important points include:

1. Consensus **does not** mean that everyone thinks the decision is the best one possible.

2. Consensus **does** mean those opposed to the decision could choose to:

   > **stand aside** - "I don't want this, but I won't block others from doing or having it."
   > **block** - "I won't support this and won't allow the group to have it."
   > **withdraw** - "I see everyone else wants this and I can't accept it. I'm willing to leave the group."

3. Consensus **does** allow for creative solutions, considering collective energy often discovers more options than does an individual.

4. Consensus **does not** mean majority rules.

5. Consensus **does not** mean win/lose. If people leave the group session feeling as if they "lost," the process needs to be discussed again.

6. Consensus **does** mean more of a time commitment than does "voting."

7. Consensus **does** mean group members need to have a commitment to negotiate compromise and present their positions assertively in order for the process to work well.

8. Consensus **does** mean group members need to encourage others to present their positions and demonstrate respect for individual ideas.

9. Consensus **does** require that the group setting remain safe with only quality feedback given, i.e., no barbs or coercion.

10. Consensus **does** mean the facilitator monitors an "equal time" policy, usually one minute per person to speak to the issue.

Personal Contract

TRANSFER

OBJECTIVE

Group members will complete personal contracts to demonstrate a commitment to using assertive and cooperative skills in their daily lives.

MATERIALS

Contracts (Experience 7.13), journals

PROCEDURE

Group members are given contract sheets (Experience 7.13) and are instructed to complete them and insert them in their journals. The personal contract is designed to give members a gentle push toward making a commitment to use assertive and cooperative actions in their lives, thus contributing to more peaceful exchange on many levels.

The self-confidence fostered in the previous assertive, cooperative exercises prepares group members for the less comfortable interactions which are important "teachers" in the human experience. In the next sections, titled "Handling Barbs" and "Recovering from Disappointments," members draw upon the storehouse of skills and inner resources developed thus far in People Skills training.

PERSONAL CONTRACT

I commit to using assertive and cooperative skills in my daily life. One setting I know this would benefit is

_____

_____

_____.

One relationship I know could benefit from assertive behavior on my part is

_____

_____

_____.

An assertive tool I like is

_____

_____

_____.

I am going to try consensual decision-making with

_____

_____about_____

_____.

NAME _____ DATE _____

NOTES (to be jotted down whenever assertive/cooperative action is tried):

_____

_____

_____

FACILITATOR LOG

Things to remember:

_____

_____

_____

_____

_____

_____

_____

_____

_____

_____

_____

_____

_____

_____

_____

_____

_____

_____

_____

_____

_____

_____

Handling
Barbs

Chapter 8

Handling Barbs

Another challenge for group members, for people in general, is learning to deal with input from others which is perceived to be hurtful. Actions sometimes described as being examples of physical or verbal abuse are labeled "barbs" in group. The visual images of thorns or the sharp points on barbed wire fences remind group members that barbs are those things people say and do that pierce through protections, giving rise to painful emotional responses.

In "Handling Barbs" activities, group members are guided to consider the themes of **perception** and **protection**. As receivers of barbs, members are invited to explore how their **perception** of what happens between people is colored by personal feelings of self-worth and by past experience. Members consider the "hows" and "whys" of **protecting themselves** from hurts through continuing self-growth activities.

Two other themes looked at are **intention** and **introspection vs. reaction**. As senders of barbs group members are asked to work with what is **really intended** in a given exchange. Most often, senders are attempting to release some strong feelings bottled up inside themselves. The fact that someone feels pain as a result of the action is secondary to the primary goal of release. Since most often the **intention** isn't to hurt someone else but to help oneself, group members are given tools to achieve this relief without reacting to the urge for a quick fix at someone else's expense.

I. **PURPOSE** -- to assist group members in identifying and handling barbs while they discover possible underlying meanings

Perception Of Barbs
AWARENESS

OBJECTIVE

Group members will brainstorm a list of common barbs heard or felt.

MATERIALS

Chart paper, marking pens

PROCEDURE

The facilitator labels the chart paper as follows:

BARB PERCEPTIONS	
PHYSICAL	VERBAL

Group members are instructed to freely brainstorm any barbs they-or people they know-have experienced, heard, or seen. In a follow-up discussion group members consider:

1. Ways they have tried to handle these barbs in the past.
2. How they felt about what was said or done.
3. What they think the other person was really trying to say, i.e., "You fool!" could mean "I feel jealous because you had a better idea than I did."
4. Why did the barb affect them the way it did?
5. How can they protect themselves from similar happenings?
6. How can they process the hurt they felt?

Not Accepting Barbs

PRACTICE

OBJECTIVE

Using a four-step model, group members will deliver feedback to persons close to them from whom they have received a barb.

MATERIALS

Model of four-step format for not accepting barbs (presented below), "Role-Play Situations" (Experience 8.1)

PROCEDURE

The facilitator displays the four-step model:

```
1. Cool off

2. "I don't like _____."

3. "I feel _____when

   _____."

4. "Instead of_____, I want

   _____."
```

The facilitator explains that this model is to be used selectively with those one loves and trusts.

When people do not accept a barb, they take responsibility for the discomfort felt by what was said or done. They let others hear perceptions of what was said or done. This gives those people care about an opportunity to explain what happened. By clearing issues, relationship "blocks" are avoided.

Group members are asked to act out the role-play situations in Experience 8.1 by using the four-step model. For example:

1. Cool off
2. "I don't like it when you whistle at me and make faces."
3. "I feel irritated and hurt when you whistle at me and make those silly faces."
4. "Instead of whistling and making faces, I want you to leave me alone."

After the role plays, a discussion follows:

1. How did you feel when you were able to clear with your partner?
2. Did you feel safe expressing yourself in this way? Why or why not?
3. With whom could you use this model?
4. When would you choose to **not** use this approach?

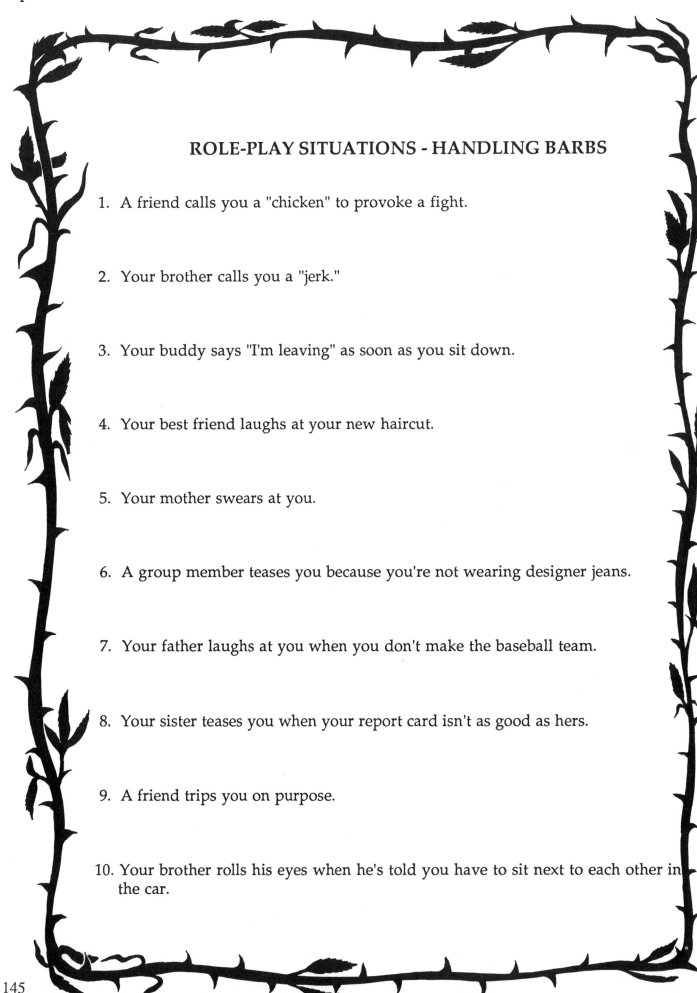

ROLE-PLAY SITUATIONS - HANDLING BARBS

1. A friend calls you a "chicken" to provoke a fight.

2. Your brother calls you a "jerk."

3. Your buddy says "I'm leaving" as soon as you sit down.

4. Your best friend laughs at your new haircut.

5. Your mother swears at you.

6. A group member teases you because you're not wearing designer jeans.

7. Your father laughs at you when you don't make the baseball team.

8. Your sister teases you when your report card isn't as good as hers.

9. A friend trips you on purpose.

10. Your brother rolls his eyes when he's told you have to sit next to each other in the car.

This Is Who I Am

MORE PRACTICE

OBJECTIVE

Group members will draw or paint a picture representative of their peaceful, centered self.

MATERIALS

Drawing paper, paints, felt pens

PROCEDURE

The facilitator leads a discussion about the importance of growing strong in the knowledge of "who you really are." Group members are guided to realize that one solid protection against barbs from others is to have a secure knowledge of one's value. The more clearly people remember the truth of the peaceful, centered persons they really are, the less likely the actions of others will shake the equilibrium and bring discomfort.

Group members are asked to sit quietly with bodies loose and relaxed. When comfortable, they are asked to close or cover their eyes and focus within themselves. The facilitator reads the following:

"Take a walk in your mind's eye, in your imagination. The path is smooth stone. Cheerful flowers and arched trees line the way. A cool breeze feels fresh against your face and the smells of wildflowers and herbs dance lightly in the air. The music of animals adds to the perfect calm of your walk. You move easily, happily toward a clearing that feels as if it's right in the center of your being. Look all around you. Notice how everything looks, smells, sounds. Pick a piece of sweet grass and taste it. Realize how at peace you are here in this center of yourself. 'This is who I am. This is how I feel about me,' you hear yourself say. 'I know the wonderful valuable being I am.'"

The facilitator allows for a few moments of silence. Group members then are asked to open their eyes and paint, draw, or write about the peaceful, centered, unshakeable place within them. These images are shared in a follow-up discussion/viewing. Group members are asked to consider how this approach to handling barbs is different from the four-step model practiced in the previous session.

Journal Writing - Barbs

TRANSFER

OBJECTIVE

Group members will log information about barbs they've experienced.

MATERIALS

Journals

PROCEDURE

The facilitator asks group members to write down barbs that are directed toward them or others during the upcoming week. They are asked to note how the barbs seemed to be perceived by the receiver and in what manner they were handled. Finally, members are asked to guess the intention of the person sending the barb: What was that person really trying to say? Members are asked to bring journals to the next meeting and share entries.

II. **PURPOSE** -- to help group members discover approaches to discharging internal stress without hurting others

Blocking

AWARENESS

OBJECTIVE

Group members will identify tension-reducing activities one could do in lieu of saying or doing something to hurt another.

MATERIALS

Chalkboard or chart paper, chalk or felt pens

PROCEDURE

The facilitator writes out the following information on a chalkboard or chart:

FEELING	REACTION BARB	BLOCKING ACTIVITY
Angry or scared	1. Hit, kick, fight 2. Swear	
Jealous	3. Name-calling (You jerk!) 4. Humiliate (I can't believe you don't get it!)	
Sad or hurt	5. Abandon (I'm not your friend anymore.)	

Members are guided to brainstorm activities they could do instead of the habitual hurtful reactions listed on the chart. All blocking activities mentioned are recorded on the chart. The group discusses the probable effectiveness of each idea.

Timeout/Look Inside
PRACTICE

OBJECTIVE

Group members will practice two introspective exercises to help them block barbs they might consider sending in the future.

MATERIALS

Contemplative, instrumental music tape; colored pens and drawing paper; Look Inside! (Experience 8.2)

PROCEDURE 1

Group members are asked to assume the body posture of someone who is upset: angry, sad, jealous, hurt, scared, or other feeling. They are instructed to silently say "I feel (**feeling word**)" until they remember the sensations of that emotion. Next, they are guided to choose a comfortable, private place in the room to sit or lie down and to breathe deeply (in through the nose, out through the mouth). Five to ten minutes is given to this steady breathing. Music may be added to the background. Members are asked to return to the group and share how this timeout exercise affected their heavy mood. They are asked to share any thoughts or imaginings they had while breathing and tuning in to themselves.

PROCEDURE 2

Group members are asked to repeat the timeout process from Procedure 1. This time, after two or three minutes of continuous breathing, the facilitator asks each to imagine an object or symbol that represents calm, peace, harmony, balance, or similar feeling. This could be a natural or artificial object or something made up. When each member has one in mind, paper and pens are distributed. Members are asked first to draw a large circle outline on the paper and then to place their special object right in the middle of the circle. The facilitator tells how a **mandala**, which means circle in Sanskrit, is a circular drawing where all designs radiate from a center much like petals on a flower or the iris of the human eye. Group members are instructed to draw shapes, lines, figures, or other forms coming from this central symbol. The symbol represents the peaceful self within. Members are encouraged to use colors attractive to them.

Music is played to add to the quiet, focused, introspective nature of the drawing.

Mandalas are shared, displayed, and discussed. Group members are asked to share how they felt creating their mandala and "looking inside" to get the central symbol or object. The facilitator points out how these types of introspective experiences allow people to work through their own inner conflict to be in a better "space" to interact with others without sending barbs (Mandala Sample, Experience 8.2).

Look Inside!

Color Combination

TRANSFER

OBJECTIVE

Group members will use two colors to help them resolve upset feelings.

MATERIALS

Journals, colored pens

PROCEDURE

Group members are instructed to choose a marker with a color to represent an upset feeling frequently experienced. Next, each is asked to select a marker to stand for a peaceful, balanced, loving feeling-a color that really makes that member feel good. On a journal page, participants are to scribble in the "upset" color and on another scribble/doodle in the "pleasant" color. Finally, each is asked to draw for a third time using both colors, with the pleasant color completely surrounding the upset color. Finally, members are instructed to ask the upset color to talk to the pleasant color to tell it

1. Why I'm upset
2. How you can help

These entries are discussed at the beginning of the next meeting.

The tools practiced in this section allow group members to release barbs put forth by others or life events without attaching to them and creating internal conflict. At times this release won't occur and individuals find themselves dealing with strong feelings and stress. The following chapter, "Recovering from Disappointments," offers options for coping with life's harder lessons/"teachers."

FACILITATOR LOG

Things to remember:

_____

_____

_____

_____

_____

_____

_____

_____

_____

_____

_____

_____

_____

_____

_____

_____

_____

_____

_____

_____

_____

_____

Recovering from
Disappointments

Chapter 9

Recovering From Disappointments

Recovering from perceived mistakes, disappointments or losses can be a difficult process. In this section, group members explore how expectations and judgments create the perception of experiences as being "mistakes," "disappointments," or "failures." Members also learn to recognize and accept strong feelings accompanying life experiences, which accelerate healing the hurts resulting from these perceived disappointments. Group members identify feelings, such as anger, fear, and sorrow. They practice how to safely and effectively deliver strong feelings to allow emotional release. Members experience stress-reduction exercises and the sense of belonging provided by a support group of peers.

I. **PURPOSE** -- to help group members become more aware of how "hard" people tend to be on themselves and begin to evaluate life experiences as being "teachers"

Judge Not

AWARENESS

OBJECTIVE

Group members will consider a list of life events often judged to be disappointing, negative, or undesirable and will brainstorm what could be learned from each.

MATERIALS

Judge Not sheets (Experiences 9.1, 9.2), pencils

PROCEDURE

Group members are given the Judge Not sheets and join together in triads to discuss and complete them. The facilitator guides members toward perceiving the experiences as learning events. Members are asked to **evaluate** the experiences according to learning potential rather than **judge** them as being OK or not OK. The facilitator guides a closing discussion by using the questions listed at the bottom of the experience sheet.

JUDGE NOT
LEVEL I

Directions: Next to each listed life experience, write anything you think of that you could learn from the experience. Number one is completed as a sample.

LIFE EVENT	LEARNINGS
1. Death of a pet	1. I'll always love my pet whether alive or not. I learned about death for the first time. I felt very sad. Crying helped. Everyone was kind to me.
2. Parents' divorce	2.
3. Fail a test	3.
4. Aren't invited to a party	4.
5. A friend chooses to be with another friend more than you	5.

Follow-up discussion questions:

1. How would life be better for you if you stopped judging experiences as "good" or "bad"?

2. Have you ever accepted a hard circumstance in your life without being too tough on yourself?

JUDGE NOT
LEVEL II

Directions: Next to each life event listed, write what lesson it may have held for the person having the experience. Think about knowledge gained, people contacts, feelings expressed, life changes. This exercise requires a real shift in usual thinking patterns. Be creative! Don't judge! Number one is a sample.

LIFE EVENT	POSSIBLE LEARNINGS
1. Death of a family member	1. Considered spiritual beliefs Experienced deep sorrow. Surviving family members came together. Recalled wonderful experiences with deceased person. Experienced the cycle of life.
2. Loss of a prized possession	2.
3. Failure to gain a desired goal	3.
4. Failure to develop the kind of relationship desired with someone	4.
5. Disappointment with performance of a particular task	5.

Follow-up discussion questions:

1. How would our lives be enhanced by dropping "good"/"bad" judgments of our life experiences?
2. What feelings would you have more frequently and less frequently by eliminating harsh judgments of life experiences?
3. All life experiences have a purpose. What does that mean to you? Do you believe that is true?

Talk-To-Me Pictures
PRACTICE

OBJECTIVE

Group members will create abstract drawings of life experiences they have previously judged to be negative. They will utilize the drawings to learn from the events instead.

MATERIALS

Drawing paper, multicolored felt pens or watercolors

PROCEDURE

The facilitator asks group members to pause and reflect upon a life experience each has **judged** to be a failure, a disappointment, or a mistake. Members are asked to particularly focus on feelings accompanying the circumstance. Next, members are instructed to choose colored pens or paints which are attractive to them. They create a representation of the event using designs, doodles, scribbles, abstract forms, and as many colors as they intuitively feel they need. When the pictures are complete, group members select one aspect of the picture with which to have a dialogue. They ask that part questions, such as:

1. Who or what are you?
2. How are you feeling?
3. What can you tell me about this experience which seemed so difficult to me?
4. What do your form and color mean?
5. Can I learn something from you?

These questions can be answered aloud or in writing. Exercises such as this are repeated several times until participants are at ease and don't limit free expression. The facilitator may ask members just to scribble and doodle without any purpose as a warm-up to this exercise.

Journal Tales
TRANSFER

OBJECTIVE

Group members will write a fairy tale, incorporating a real-life "hard experience" and will create a positive outcome.

MATERIALS

Journals, pens or pencils

PROCEDURE

Group members are asked to select a life experience which has felt difficult for them. Each creates a fairy tale which incorporates this real-life event as the crisis of the story. The crisis is resolved in the tale as the writer imagines possible positive outcomes-perhaps in the form of something learned by the main character. The facilitator stresses again that it is possible to stop judging and dismissing certain experiences as being undesirable and to start viewing all life events as important "teachers." Stories are shared at the beginning of the next group meeting.

II. **PURPOSE** -- to help group members identify the behavioral indicators of strong feelings

Feeling Emotions
AWARENESS

OBJECTIVE

Group members will brainstorm descriptors of the feelings of anger, fear, and sorrow and discuss events which elicit these feelings.

MATERIALS

Chart paper, felt pens

PROCEDURE

The facilitator lists the headings "Anger," "Fear," and "Sorrow" on three separate pieces of chart paper and draws a line down the middle of each chart. Recorders are selected for each of the listed feelings. The right column is used for listing life events which elicit each of the feelings, e.g., Sorrow: someone you love dies, your boyfriend breaks up with you, you aren't selected for a position you really wanted. The left column is used to describe physical sensations and behaviors a person demonstrates when experiencing each feeling, e.g., Anger: red face, hot face, hot, sweaty, yelling, hitting. Group members are directed to brainstorm for all categories at once. Such a "buzz" of ideas breaks down inhibitions and encourages quality input.

Strong Feelings Scripts

PRACTICE

OBJECTIVE

Group members label feelings and behaviors which demonstrate those feelings after listening to two short scripts.

MATERIALS

Strong Feelings Scripts (Experiences 9.3, 9.4)

PROCEDURE

Group members are asked to volunteer to read the Strong Feelings scripts. The first reading is uninterrupted. During the second reading, the facilitator stops the action periodically to ask how the group thinks a character is feeling and how they came to this decision, i.e., what behaviors told them a character was feeling a certain way.

STRONG FEELINGS SCRIPT #1

Identify strong feelings and how different people demonstrate them.

Narrator: The scene is the home of Mr. King, who is a single parent raising his three sons-Matt, Jonathan, and Chris. Mr. King's girlfriend is coming for dinner. He is rushing, trying to get prepared, and is behind schedule.

Mr. King: OK guys! Stop watching TV right now! I told you to help and I mean it!

Matt: Oh brother, more work! (He turns the TV up louder and ignores his dad.)

Mr. King: Turn that off! Two of you do the dishes and one of you vacuum.

Chris: I get to vacuum.

Matt: No, I do. You always get to do it. (pushes Chris)

Chris: You creep! (shoves Matt, who falls over a chair)

Jonathan: He's bleeding! He's bleeding! He's really hurt! (starts to cry)

Chris: I'm really sorry, Matt. (His face is white.)

Mr. King: (walks in, sees the mess, and clenches his fists) What happened?

Jonathan: Boy, are we going to get it! (runs and locks himself in the bathroom)

Chris: I'm sorry, Dad. (puts his hand on Matt's shoulder and lowers his head)

Matt: Do I need stitches, Dad? (hands shaking)

Mr. King: We better go have someone check it out. (doorbell rings)

Narrator: Mr. King's girlfriend walks in, opens her mouth, and freezes at the sight before her.

Discussion questions:
1. How do you think Mr. King is feeling as he tries to get ready for dinner with his girlfriend?
2. How do Mr. King's boys react when their dad asks them for help?
3. How do Jonathan and Chris express their feelings after Matt gets hurt?
4. How does Mr. King's girlfriend display her feelings when she enters the room?

STRONG FEELINGS SCRIPT # 2

Identify the strong feelings and how different people demonstrate them.

Narrator: Ms. James is driving home from work with news which will affect her family. Her boss has asked her to travel to several conventions which will take her away from her family for days at a time. She imagined the reactions of her husband Kyle and her daughters, Gina and Camilla.

Ms. James: (at the dinner table) I have some news for everyone. (Her voice is low and she clears her throat.) I have been asked to attend a series of conventions this year. That will mean traveling two to three days some weeks. (She searches their faces.)

Camilla: That will mean more baby sitters. I hate baby sitters, and I hate you! (cries)

Mr. James: I think it sounds exciting. (His voice was quiet and he picked at his food.)

Camilla: Exciting? It's lousy news! (throws her spoon down and races out of the room)

Gina: Who's going to take me to dance lessons and soccer practice on those days? Do I have to give that up? (She was wringing her napkin.)

Ms. James: No, of course not. We'll work that all out, or I won't accept the position. Come on, I need everyone's cooperation. (pleading voice)

Mr. James: (sits back and sighs) This is going to be hard on me.

Ms. James: (covers her face and nods her head back and forth)

Gina: Cheer up, Mom. (pats her arm)

Discussion questions:

1. How is each of the family members feeling about Ms. James's news?
2. How does each display emotional reaction?
3. What could you suggest each person do next?
4. Can you relate to the reactions of any particular family member?

Feelings In Pictures
TRANSFER

OBJECTIVE

Group members will identify feeling states by reading body language.

MATERIALS

Magazine pictures of people demonstrating a variety of strong feelings, journals

PROCEDURE

The facilitator gives each group member a "people picture" at the end of a group meeting. Group members are instructed to write a statement in their journals about how the person is feeling and what they think happened to bring about the particular feeling state. These entries are shared during the next meeting.

III. **PURPOSE** -- to assist group members in releasing strong feelings in order to gain from experiencing them

Ways Of Discharging Strong Feelings
AWARENESS

OBJECTIVE

Group members will state effective ways of discharging strong feelings.

MATERIALS

Chart paper and felt pens

PROCEDURE

The facilitator leads a discussion on ways to discharge strong feelings, such as anger, fear, sorrow, and envy. Group members are invited to brainstorm ways they discharge these feelings. The facilitator emphasizes that all suggestions are not to be judged or evaluated. The facilitator may use the four strong feelings suggested above or any other feeling words that are appropriate to the group. The chart paper is divided into four equal sections, and one of the feeling words is written in each section. The brainstormed ideas are written in the appropriate sections. Once the brainstorming is finished, the facilitator asks any of the following questions:

1. Which ideas would be helpful to you in discharging strong feelings?
2. Which ideas are ones you use regularly when expressing your feelings?
3. Is there a suggestion that feels uncomfortable to you?
4 If you aren't satisfied with the way you deal with your strong feelings now, are there any suggestions you heard today which might be beneficial to you?

Dealing With Fear

PRACTICE

OBJECTIVE

Group members will experiment with different ways of dealing with their fears.

MATERIALS

Drawing paper, crayons, felt pens, paints, brushes, journals, pencils

PROCEDURE

The facilitator begins the activity by having group members share some of their fears. After the sharing, the facilitator explains that people are often told they should not be afraid; they should be brave. By talking, writing, or drawing what is frightening, people confront the things they fear instead of denying or avoiding them. Group members choose two or more of the following ways to deal with their fears:

1. Draw a picture of something that frightens you.
2. Write about all the things that scare you.
3. Write a poem about being afraid.
4. Write about what you do when you're afraid.
5. Draw a picture of yourself being afraid. The drawing might include the person, thing, or situation that "touches off" the fear. Draw a second picture in which there is a happy ending. This picture shows how the fear was "befriended." If members feel comfortable, they share drawings or writings.

Dealing With Anger
MORE PRACTICE

OBJECTIVE

Group members will practice ways to discharge anger.

MATERIALS

Drawing paper, felt pens, crayons, paints, brushes, journals, pencils

PROCEDURE

The facilitator begins the activity by leading a discussion of the kinds of things that bring forth anger. Group members brainstorm a list of things to which they respond in anger. The facilitator explains that anger is released in many different ways, such as in pictures, in writing, in speech, and through movement. Group members are asked to try several of the following ways to discharge anger:

1. Choose a color or colors that look "angry" to you. Draw or scribble angry pictures. Try many angry scribbles.
2. Write about your angry feelings. Any words are OK. No one will read what you write unless you give permission.
3. Lie on a bed or floor, clench your fists and pound the bed, floor or pillows. If you feel the need, scream or yell while you are pounding. Before doing this, check to see that you are in safe surroundings. Consider having a friend nearby when you do this activity.
4. Use an inanimate object, i.e., punching bag, soft padded bat, or knotted towel, to discharge anger. When using the knotted towel or padded bat, raise the object above your head and swing the object down hard onto a pillow. The noise made as the bat or towel moves through the air contributes to the emotional release.

Dealing With Sadness
STILL MORE PRACTICE

OBJECTIVE

Group members will express sadness by drawing or writing about a time they felt sad.

MATERIALS

Drawing paper, crayons, felt pens, paints, brushes, journals, pencils

PROCEDURE

The facilitator leads a discussion of the types of things that lead to feelings of sadness or sorrow. The facilitator explains that most people are taught to hide or deny sadness. "Don't cry" is a phrase heard frequently, indicating that crying is not acceptable. Group discussion emphasizes that sorrow is a natural emotion. When people allow themselves to experience sadness, that expression helps them develop compassion and understanding for self and others and to experience joy more fully. Group members are asked to choose one or more of the following activities to help process feelings of sorrow:

1. Draw a picture that depicts sadness. Choose colors that are meaningful to you in the expression of sorrow.
2. Write about the picture.
3. Write a poem about a sad experience. The poem could begin with "I feel sad when...." or "When I'm sad, I...."
4. Sit down and tell a close friend about a time you felt sad.

Release Letters

TRANSFER

OBJECTIVE

Group members will write letters to people with whom they have unresolved issues.

MATERIALS

Journals, paper, pencils

PROCEDURE

The facilitator instructs group members to think of someone with whom they have been unable to resolve a conflict. They are asked to write a letter to that person and tell exactly how they feel. The intent of the letter writing is to provide a release of emotion. It is an opportunity to "let go" of held resentments, anger, hurts, and other strong feelings. The letter is not meant to be mailed; rather, it serves as a tool for processing blocked emotions. Blocked emotion keeps people from being able to communicate freely and resolve conflicts.

IV. **PURPOSE** -- to assist group members in determining when and how to deliver strong feelings to others

Brainstorming Possible Delivery Methods

AWARENESS

OBJECTIVE

Group members will discuss guidelines for effective clearing of emotions and brainstorm pitfalls for each guideline.

MATERIALS

Chart paper or chalkboard, felt pens or chalk

PROCEDURE

GUIDELINES FOR EFFECTIVE CLEARING OF EMOTIONS	PITFALLS (Samples)
1. Focus on behaviors not people.	1. (attacking a person with words....)
2. Use "I" statements, i.e., "own" your emotions.	2. (blaming someone....)
3. Be brief and stay focused on current circumstances.	3. (dredging up old annoyances....)
4. Use assertive (not aggressive) body language.	4. (trying to clear when still really "plugged in"....)
5. Allow others to contribute their perspectives.	5. (lambasting others with no regard for their feelings....)
6. Consider your motivation.	6. (hurting someone, "paybacks"....)
7. Consider your expectations.	7. (expecting agreement or apology....)
8. Ask if the other person will listen to you.	8. (catching someone off guard, setting yourself up to be rejected....)

The facilitator writes out the "guidelines" side of the chart (above) prior to the group meeting. Group members discuss each guideline and consider if and why each is helpful. Next to each guideline the facilitator records any potential pitfalls group members think of related to each guideline. Sample pitfalls are noted in parentheses on the chart.

Clearing Strong Feelings
PRACTICE

OBJECTIVE

Group members will express strong feelings, using "I" statements in role-play situations.

MATERIALS

Role-play situations (Experiences 9.5, 9.6)

PROCEDURE

Group members take turns reading the role-play situations and completing the "I" statement section. Several group members are asked to do the same role-play situation. This demonstrates how different people may react to the same situation with dissimilar or similar emotion. The facilitator also asks group members to consider the following before clearing strong feelings with other people:

1. What is my motivation for clearing this strong feeling? (Possibilities: I want to feel better, I want us to have honest communication, I want that person to feel badly for hurting me, I just want to be heard.)
2. What are my expectations for the clearing? (Possibilities: I expect an apology, I don't expect anything, I just need to air my feelings, I expect that person to be a good listener, I expect that one to be rude to me.)
3. How will you feel if your expectations aren't met? What will you do then?
4. Are there other ways to process the emotions involved without including anyone else? What are some ways? (Consider ideas from the "Discharging Emotions" section.)
5. When would be a circumstance in which you might not choose to deliver a strong feeling to another but would process the emotions in a different way?

The facilitator continues to guide group members toward taking responsibility for their emotions and learning from experiencing them as opposed to blocking expression of them.

DELIVERING STRONG FEELINGS
Role-Play Situations #1

1. Julie was invited to Tara's birthday party. Julie's best friend, Amy, wasn't invited and she has been avoiding Julie. Julie calls Amy on the phone and says:

   I'd like to talk to you about something that's been bothering me. Can you listen to me now?
   I don't like it when _____.
   I feel _____.
   I want _____.

2. Frank is upset because his classmate, Rob, has been teasing him about his new haircut. Frank goes up to Rob and says:

   I'd like to talk to you about something that's been bothering me. Would you give me a minute?
   I don't like it when _____.
   I feel _____.
   I want _____.

3. Brianna, Valerie, and Jessica have been best friends for two years. Last week Brianna and Valerie began teasing Jessica and leaving her out of their games. Jessica goes up to her friends and says:

   I'd like to talk to you about something that's been bothering me. Can we sit down together for a while?
   I don't like it when _____.
   I feel _____.
   I want _____.

4. Kate has three brothers and two sisters. She is upset because her mom never has time to be alone with her. She really needs to talk to her mom about something personal. She goes up to her mom and says:

   I'd like to talk to you about something that's been bothering me. When would you have time to listen?
   I don't like it when _____.
   I feel _____.
   I want _____.

5. Larry has a vision problem and has to wear thick glasses. In class Christina giggles at him and calls him "four-eyes." He sees her alone at recess and says:

   I'd like to talk to you about something that's been bothering me. Do you have time to listen?
   I don't like it when _____.
   I feel _____.
   I want _____.

DELIVERING STRONG FEELINGS
Role-Play Situations #2

1. Annie was accepted into a training program. Her best friend wasn't chosen and has been avoiding Annie. On the phone Annie says:

   I'd like to talk to you about something that's been bothering me. Do you have a minute?
   I don't like it when _____.
   I feel _____.
   I want _____.

2. Karl knows his friend Jim is an alcoholic. He goes to Jim's house and asks him to go for a walk. He says:

   I'd like to talk to you about something that's been bothering me. Is this a good time?
   I don't like it when _____.
   I feel _____.
   I want _____.

3. Jason overhears someone he asked out laughing about him to her friend. He sees her alone and says:

   I'd like to talk to you about something that's been bothering me. Do you have time to listen?
   I don't like it when _____.
   I feel _____.
   I want _____.

4. Jessie is working on a group project with five others. They seem to reject all of her ideas and even seem to be shutting her out of conversations. She asks everyone to stop for a moment and says:

   I'd like to talk to you about something that's been bothering me. Can you all listen to me for a moment?
   I don't like it when _____.
   I feel _____.
   I want _____.

5. Bill has grown up with a hearing loss which affects his speech. Mary giggles when he talks in class. He sees her sitting alone at the bus stop and says:

   I'd like to talk to you about something that's been bothering me. May I sit down and tell you now?
   I don't like it when _____.
   I feel _____.
   I want _____.

Clearing In Real Life

TRANSFER

OBJECTIVE

Group members will apply guidelines for delivering strong feelings to real-life situations.

MATERIALS

Journals, paper, pencils

PROCEDURE

In between group meetings, members are asked to utilize information learned in the previous sections. Any strong feelings experienced are processed, using discharge and/or delivery suggestions. Members are asked to record examples and share these at the beginning of subsequent group meetings.

V. **PURPOSE** -- to demonstrate to members the importance of maintaining a balance between stress and support

Stress/Support Scale
AWARENESS

OBJECTIVE

Group members will determine the levels of stress and support in their lives.

MATERIALS

Stress and support scales (Experiences 9.7, 9.8)

PROCEDURE

The facilitator distributes the stress and support scales, explains how to complete them and assists with questions which may arise. When the papers are finished, participants discuss issues relating to stress and support. Questions to spark discussion include:

1. How are strong feelings-such as fear, anger, sorrow-connected to stress?
2. How is stress reduced through the discharge of strong feelings?
3. What part does a support network play in reducing stress?
4. Who are the people in your support network?
5. What are you doing about the stress level in your life?

STRESS SCALE**

This exercise will help you measure how much stress you have had during the last year. It will also show you how important other people can be in helping you deal with stress. New medical studies show that people who have close friends and family have less mental and physical illness than people who try to go it alone.

Circle each stress event that happened to you within the last 12 months. Circle the items that are starred (*) only if the event happened more than twice during the year. Add the scores for each item circled and put the total on the line.

PERSONAL

(6)   Serious injury or illness
(6)   Alcohol, drug or emotional problem
(4)   Death of close friend
(2)   * Trouble with friends or neighbors   Total _____

EDUCATION

(4)   Skipped a grade, stayed back a grade, lost a job position, or were promoted at work
(4)   Changed schools or jobs
(2)   * Trouble with teacher or class subject, trouble with boss or work expectations

Total _____

FAMILY

(10) Death of parent or immediate family member
(8)   Divorce in family
(6)   Separation or reconciliation in family
(6)   New stepmother, stepfather, or stepchild
(4)   Serious illness or injury of family member
(4)   Birth or adoption of sister, brother, or child
(4)   New stepbrother or stepsister
(4)   Brother, sister, or child leaves home
(4)   Relative moves into household
(4)   Moved to new house
(4)   * Family arguments   Total _____

TOTAL STRESS SCORE _____

IF YOUR STRESS LEVEL SCORE IS

Less than 10:   You have a low stress level. You have few stressors with which to deal.

10-15   You have a moderate (or medium) stress level. There has been a lot of change in your life.

16 or more   You have a high stress level. There have been major adjustments in your life. This type of stress is harmful, especially if it lasts a long time.

** Used with permission from California Department of Mental Health. Adapted from *Mental Health:The Youth Award Handbook*, the Mental Health Association, Los Angeles, California, 1982.

SUPPORT NETWORK SCALE **

Circle one response for each item. Then add the scores next to each item you circled and put the total in the box.

1. How many persons do you talk to about a school/work problem?

   (0) none
   (3) one
   (4) two or three
   (5) four or more   Total _____

2. How many friends do you trade favors with, such as loan items, share meals, help with tasks?

   (0) none
   (1) one
   (2) two or three
   (3) four or more   Total _____

3. Do you have a close friend or best friend?

   (0) no
   (2) several different friends
   (6) one steady friend
   (10) many friends, one best friend Total _____

4. How often do friends and close family members visit you at home?

   (0) rarely
   (1) about once a month
   (4) several times a month
   (8) once a week or more   Total _____

5. How many friends or family members do you talk to about personal matters?

   (0) none
   (6) one or two
   (8) three to five
   (10) six or more   Total _____

6. How often do you participate in a social, community or sports group?

   (0) rarely
   (1) about once a month
   (2) once a week or more   Total _____

TOTAL SUPPORT SCALE _____

IF YOUR SUPPPORT NETWORK SCORE IS

Less than 10:   Your support network has low strength and probably does not
                provide much support. You need to consider getting closer to people.

15-29   Your support network has moderate strength and likely provides
                enough support except during periods of high stress.

30 or more: Your support network has high strength, and it will probably
                maintain your well-being even during periods of high stress.

** Used with permission from California Department of Mental Health. Adapted from *Mental Health:The Youth Award Handbook*, the Mental Health Association, Los Angeles, California, 1982.

Relaxation Techniques

PRACTICE

OBJECTIVE

Group members will practice stress reduction exercises.

MATERIALS

New Age instrumental tapes, any relaxing music group members bring to share

PROCEDURE

The facilitator introduces group members to several stress-reduction techniques to be practiced.

1. **Balloon Breathing** - While seated or lying down, group members are instructed to close their eyes and breathe as if they were asleep. The inhale pushes the stomach area up like a balloon and the exhale releases tension and deflates "the balloon." Participants are encouraged to really "blow" the tension out, even to add a vocalization to the exhale. Variation: Group members select a word which has a pleasant connotation for them. On the exhale they whisper their cue word in an attempt to eliminate negativism and replace it with peaceful energy.

2. **Guided Imagery** - Group members write fantasy situations, using many descriptors to spark visual pictures. Those who desire read their fantasies to music while others close their eyes and practice balloon breathing. A discussion of what each experienced and drawings of how the imaginary journey looked to different group members are used as follow-up.

3. **Progressive Relaxation** - This takes a variety of forms and basically requires group members to focus on body parts, moving from their toes to top of head. The facilitator asks members to tense body parts in succession and then release the tension. Participants can be asked to focus warmth into each body part in succession and in the end just to sit or lie and "soak up" warm energy as if they were sponges absorbing warm water.

Support Circle
MORE PRACTICE

OBJECTIVE

Group members will identify people in their lives to whom they disclose different levels of information to gain needed support.

MATERIALS

Circle of Support (Experience 9.9)

PROCEDURE

The facilitator asks group members to consider the following list of situations and decide with whom they could share the experience using the "Circle of Support" picture as a guide. They are directed to mark the situation number next to the name of the group on the circle with whom they would be comfortable sharing the experience or information.

1. Laugh really hard with....
2. Tell a big secret to....
3. Get angry with....
4. Cry in front of....
5. Ask for help from....
6. Ask directions from....
7. Ask for money from....
8. Ask for help with solving a problem....
9. Invite home....
10. Tell family problem to....

In follow-up discussion, group members suggest ways to increase support available to them.

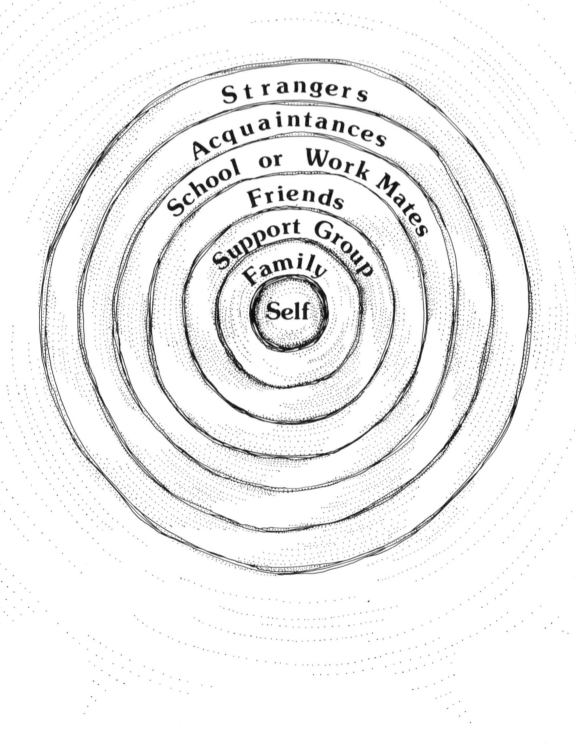

Strangers

Acquaintances

School or Work Mates

Friends

Support Group

Family

Self

Circle Of Support

Supportive Friends

TRANSFER

OBJECTIVE

Group members complete sentences, revealing information about friends as support people.

MATERIALS

Journals, list of open-ended sentences

PROCEDURE

The facilitator gives group members the following open-ended sentences to complete in their journals and share at the beginning of the next group.

1. A friendship with a peer offers _____.
2. Friendships with older people are_____.
3. Friendships with relatives are_____.
4. A friend of the opposite sex is_____.
5. Acquaintances offer_____.
6. I want to talk to_____about_____.
7. I'd never tell_____about_____.
8. I can always count on_____.
9. My greatest source of support is_____.
10. A support group offers_____.

As group members become skilled in using life experiences and the accompanying feelings as "teachers," each becomes stronger, more powerful, and self-assured. In the next chapter, titled "Solving Problems," this personal power and each person's commitment to cooperative interactions are challenged.

FACILITATOR LOG

Things to remember:

_____

_____

_____

_____

_____

_____

_____

_____

_____

_____

_____

_____

_____

_____

_____

_____

_____

_____

_____

_____

_____

_____

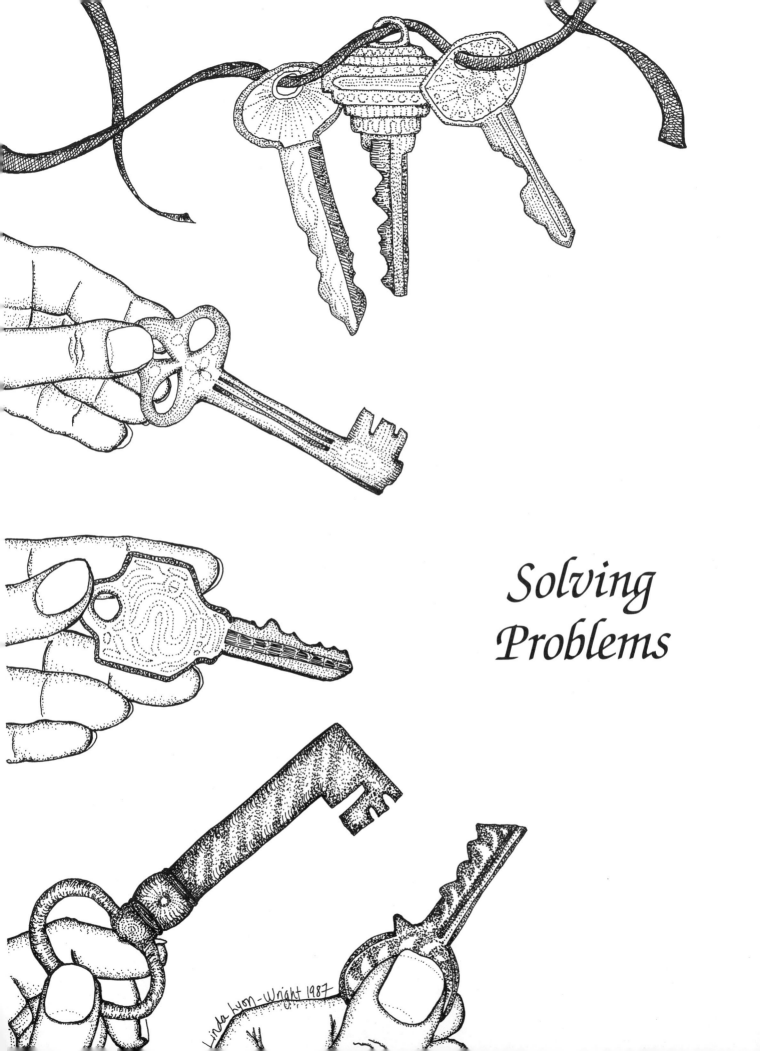

Solving
Problems

Linda Lyon-Wright 1987

Chapter 10

Solving Problems

All of the People Skills practiced so far are used to effectively solve problems. The more communication skills people acquire, the more successful their problem-solving efforts will be. In this section, group members are shown how to approach a problem as an individual. Guidance is given in seeking problem-solving help from a group of people or a trusted person, as well. Participants explore solutions to conflict situations in which two or more people agree that a problem exists. They also experiment with strategies for resolving conflicts in which only one party perceives a problem.

I. **PURPOSE** -- to present members with a problem-solving model and conflict resolution strategies** that they can use in their daily lives

Conflict In The News
AWARENESS

OBJECTIVE

Through the use of magazine articles, group members will find current news items that show conflict.

MATERIALS

Current newspaper or weekly magazines that have worldwide news articles, such as Time or Newsweek

PROCEDURE

The facilitator asks group members to go through the newspapers and/or magazines and look for articles showing conflict between two or more parties. Once members have found the articles, the facilitator leads a discussion using the following questions:

1. How do the parties in conflict know a problem exists?
2. What benefits would arise in solving the problem?
3. What are the chances that the conflict will be resolved?
4. How do you think a resolution could be reached?

Next, the facilitator asks group members to brainstorm conflicts they have in their personal lives and points out any similarities that occur.

Discussion follows as to ways that personal conflicts can be resolved. Group members are asked to envision the concept that resolving personal conflicts makes an impact on global conflict resolution. The idea that world peace "begins at home" is explored as well.

** Adapted from *A Curriculum on Conflict Management: Practical Methods for Helping Children Explore Creative Alternatives in Dealing with Conflict*, Uvaldo Palomares and Ben Logan, The Human Development Training Institute and United Methodist Communications, 1975.

Handling The Problem Yourself
PRACTICE

OBJECTIVE

Group members will be able to state the steps in the "Handling the Problem Yourself" model.

MATERIALS

Handling the Problem Yourself model (Experience 10.1), Problem Situations (Experience 10.2)

PROCEDURE

These exercises are meant to be utilized over several meetings. The "Handling the Problem Yourself" model is posted and referred to anytime a group member presents a problem to the group.

The facilitator leads the group in a discussion for each step in the "Handling the Problem Yourself" model. The following are important points to mention in this discussion:

1. **COOL OFF** -- Those who initiate the problem solving need to carefully "read" their feelings as well as others' feelings before attempting to work through the conflict. Are both parties feeling calm and ready to discuss the problem? If not, wait for a more appropriate moment. Further upset arises when one or both parties try to communicate through rage.

2. **STATE THE PROBLEM BEHAVIOR** -- All persons have an opportunity to express their feelings by making an "I don't like it when...." statement. After the first person's version of the problem is stated, that member goes on to steps 3 and 4 before the second person begins expressing feelings.

3. **STATE THE FEELING** -- The first person continues expressing feelings by stating "I feel...when...."

4. **STATE WHAT YOU WANT** -- Finally, the first person states "I want...." The person who has been listening then has an opportunity to complete steps 2, 3, and 4 before both move on to step 5.

5. **RESOLVE THE CONFLICT** -- At this point it is necessary to decide whether both parties want to continue working on the problem. If persons initiating the problem-solving attempt feel another party is being uncooperative, they may choose to drop the issue and walk away. But if both parties are actively seeking a solution, a conflict management strategy can be applied (see the following "More Practice" experience).

Once this model is understood, group members practice by completing the "Problem Situations," Experience 10.2.

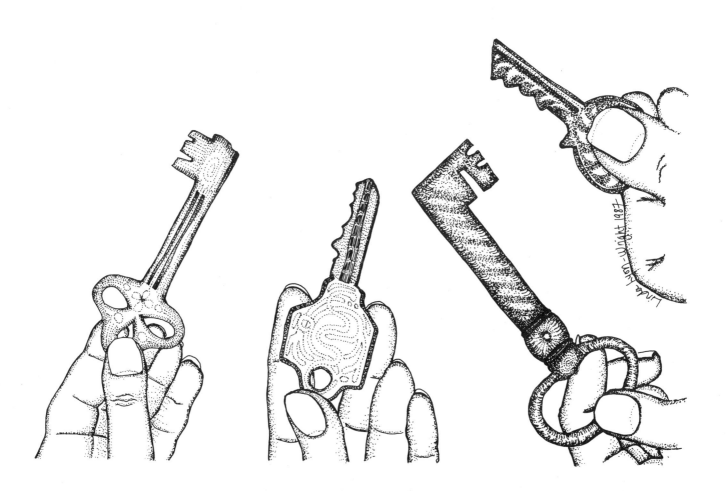

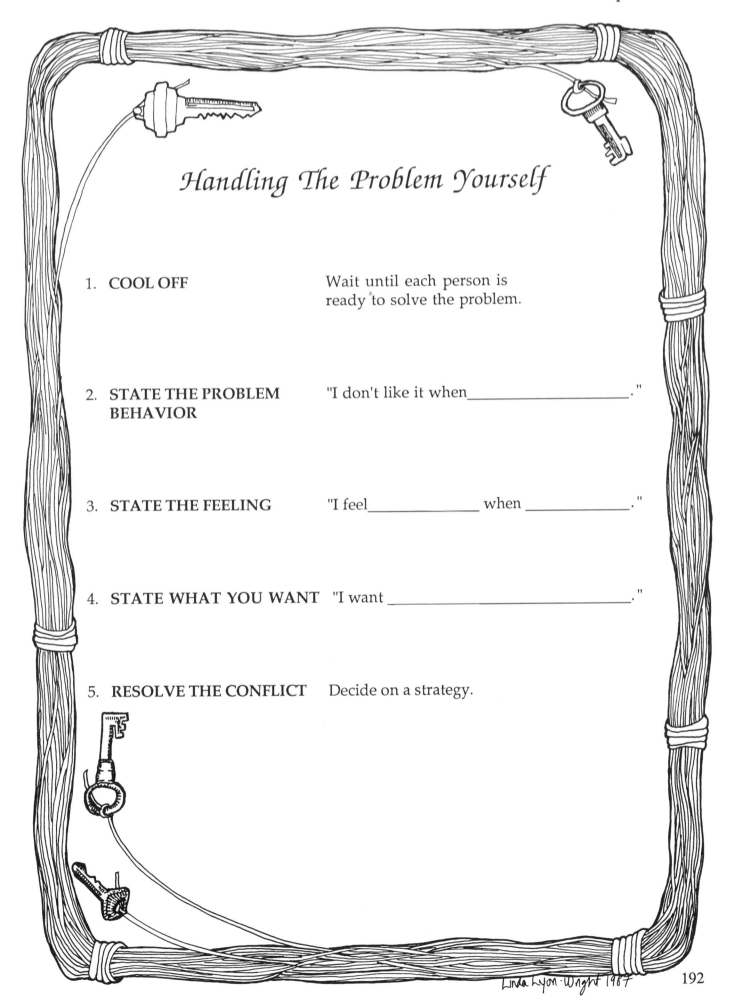

Handling The Problem Yourself

1. **COOL OFF**   Wait until each person is
                                    ready to solve the problem.

2. **STATE THE PROBLEM**   "I don't like it when_____."
   BEHAVIOR

3. **STATE THE FEELING**   "I feel_____ when _____."

4. **STATE WHAT YOU WANT**   "I want _____."

5. **RESOLVE THE CONFLICT**   Decide on a strategy.

Linda Lyon-Wright 1987

PROBLEM SITUATIONS

Read each problem. Use the Handling the Problem Yourself model to work on solving each situation.

1. Marie's parents expect her to go to college like her older brothers. She thinks she'd rather become a carpenter's apprentice. She goes to her parents and says:

   "I don't like it when_____."
   "I feel_____ when _____."
   "I want _____."

2. Joshua loaned his coat to a friend. He has asked for it to be returned without any luck. He approaches his friend and says:

   "I don't like it when_____."
   "I feel_____when _____."
   "I want _____."

3. Pam and Terri are good friends. Terri gets very jealous whenever Pam spends time with anyone else. Pam goes up to Terri and says:

   "I don't like it when_____."
   "I feel_____when _____."
   "I want _____."

4. Paul is trying to lose weight. One of his friends teases him about his weight problem. Paul lets his temper cool down before he says to his friend:

   "I don't like it when_____."
   "I feel_____when _____."
   "I want _____."

5. Jamie and Kelly share a bedroom. Jamie tends to keep her things tidy while Kelly never picks up anything. When it comes time to clean up, Jamie is expected to help until the room is clean. Jamie says to Kelly:

   "I don't like it when_____."
   "I feel_____when _____."
   "I want _____."

Linda Lyon-Wright 1987

Conflict Management Strategies

MORE PRACTICE

OBJECTIVE

Group members will discuss and become familiar with conflict management strategies.

MATERIALS

Conflict Management Strategies (Experience 10.3), Resolve the Conflict (Experience 10.4)

PROCEDURE

The facilitator leads a discussion on strategies for resolving conflicts. Experience 10.3 is used for discussing the nine strategies listed. Experience 10.4 serves as a poster to be used whenever conflict resolution or problem solving is sought.

CONFLICT MANAGEMENT STRATEGIES

1. **ABANDONING** -- leaving a situation in which resolution probably won't occur

2. **APOLOGIZING** -- saying "sorry" without necessarily implying you have said, done, believed, etc., anything wrong

3. **AVOIDING** -- deciding it's not worth the bother and "giving in" to the other person's position

4. **CHANCE** -- choosing techniques such as flipping a coin or picking a number between 1 and 10 to settle a conflict

5. **COMPROMISE** -- consenting to give up something to resolve conflict, understanding that all involved parties do the same

6. **HUMOR** -- diffusing tension around a conflict by making light of the situation in ways that take care of everyone involved

7. **POSTPONING** -- agreeing to wait for a better time to handle the conflict

8. **SEEKING HELP** -- seeking consultation or help (through inner or outer guidance) when individual efforts have failed

9. **SHARING** -- consenting to take equal responsibility for an existing conflict

Linda Lyon-Wright 1987

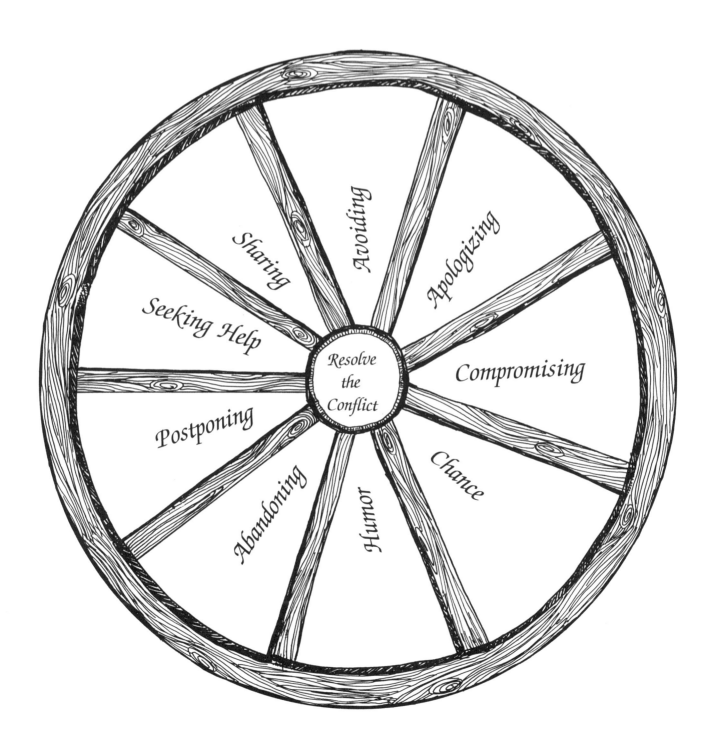

Resolutions

STILL MORE PRACTICE

OBJECTIVE

Group members will play the "Game of Resolutions."

MATERIALS

Resolution Strategy Cards (Experience 10.5)

PROCEDURE

The facilitator explains the game rules as follows:

1. Select a volunteer who is willing to share a concern or problem with the group.
2. Pass out cut-up "Resolution Strategy Cards" to remaining group members. (It is all right if some members have more than one card.)
3. Each person's role is to help the volunteer by using the strategy cards given to each member. For example: The person who receives "postponing" might suggest that the volunteer would be better off talking about the problem at a later time.
4. After about five minutes, have group members try to identify the various strategies.
5. Discussion questions:
   -- Which strategies were the easiest to deliver? The hardest to deliver?
   -- Which strategies were easy to identify? Hard to identify?
   -- Ask the volunteer how it felt receiving the suggestions. Did it help?
   -- Ask members how they felt about the suggestions they gave.

This game can be played again and again. Different group members will have opportunities to share problems.

RESOLUTION STRATEGY CARDS

ABANDONING	APOLOGIZING	AVOIDING
"If it looks as if you're not getting anywhere, you may want to walk away."	"Have you considered saying you're sorry?" or "Perhaps an apology would work."	"If it looks as if you're not going to win, you might consider giving in this time."

CHANCE	COMPROMISE	HUMOR
"Why don't you flip a coin?" or "How about drawing straws?" or "You could pick a number between 1 and 10."	"Maybe both of you could give something up to resolve the conflict."	"Have you thought about joking with the person in a friendly way?"

POSTPONING	SEEKING HELP	SHARING
"Perhaps it would be better to talk about this problem at another time."	"You might consider getting someone else to help you." or "What about going home and thinking over the whole thing."	"Couldn't you just share or take turns?"

Your Own Fairy Tale

TRANSFER

OBJECTIVE

Group members will write a fairy tale about themselves.

MATERIALS

Paper or journal, pens, pencils

PROCEDURE

The facilitator asks group members to think about a favorite fairy tale. They are asked to imagine that they are the leading character in the fairy tale and are asked to consider how it feels. (Is it exciting, frightening, delightful, fun?) If members feel comfortable, they share their thoughts about who they were and how they felt being that person.

Next, group members write an original fairy tale. They can be the lead role or any other. Each fairy tale includes the following:

1. a hero/heroine or "good" character
2. a villain or "bad" character
3. a problem
4. a resolution to the problem

The facilitator suggests that group members fictionalize a real problem they have had and "live it out" through the fantasies they create. Members bring their fairy tales to the next group meeting to share with others.

II. **PURPOSE** -- to present group members with a format for resolving conflicts with assistance

Mediation
AWARENESS

OBJECTIVE

Group members will discuss how a third-party mediator can be helpful.

MATERIALS

Large sheet of chart paper, felt pen

PROCEDURE

The facilitator asks group members to think of groups or organizations (e.g., labor unions, teachers' associations, political groups) which have conflicts. Ideas are listed on the chart paper. Next, members discuss how these groups or organizations resolve their conflicts. Hopefully, the concept of a third party or mediator will be mentioned. If not, the facilitator brings it up. Members consider the benefits of having a mediator to help both parties in resolving an existing problem. Benefits are written out on the chart paper. In closing, members consider how two or more parties in such a heated disagreement benefit from the assistance of a neutral third party. Resolutions can be reached in seemingly hopeless stalemates.

Assisted Problem-Solving

PRACTICE

OBJECTIVE

Group members will be able to state the steps in the Assisted Problem-Solving Model.

MATERIALS

Assisted Problem-Solving Model (Experience 10.6), Conflict Management Strategies (Experience 9.3)

PROCEDURE

The facilitator leads a discussion of the "Assisted Problem-Solving Model" steps. The following are important points to be mentioned in this discussion:

1. **COOL OFF** -- Make sure both parties are calm and ready to work on the problem together.

2. **TRY STEPS 2-5** -- This refers to the "Handling the Problem Yourself" model. Make sure members have tried this before coming for help. Stress that members are capable of handling the majority of their problems without assistance.

3. **STATE THE PROBLEM** -- It is important that the problem is stated very clearly.

4. **BRAINSTORM** -- Another person or other people can help with suggested strategies for solving the problem. Use of the Conflict Management Strategies (Experience 9.3) can be helpful.

5. **CONSIDER CONSEQUENCES** -- Participants are asked to write out all possible consequences for themselves or others. Next, they rate them as bringing pleasant (+) or unsettled (-) feelings to those involved in the problem. The facilitator reminds members that a problem continues to exist if unsettled feelings are present. Sometimes the unsettled feelings are unavoidable and the strategy of abandoning is necessary.

6. **TRY A SOLUTION** -- The group leader emphasizes the possibility that more than one solution may need to be tried or that a solution may need to be tried several times before resolution occurs. In other words, don't give up easily!

7. **REPORT BACK** -- There is security in knowing that someone is waiting to be supportive no matter what the outcome.

Once this model is understood, group members practice using the model with problems from their own lives, ones discussed previously or problems taken from newspapers or magazines. They fill out the bottom of Experience 10.6 and then discuss their ideas with other members.

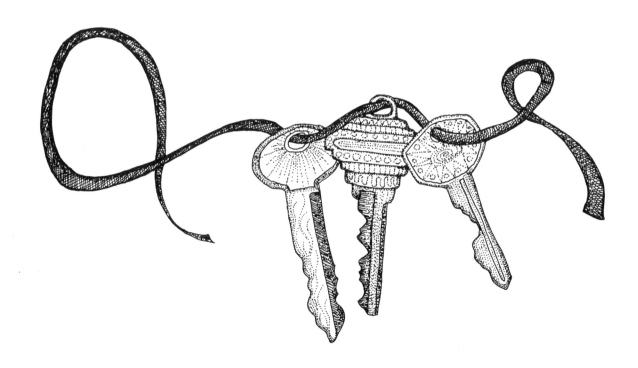

ASSISTED PROBLEM-SOLVING MODEL

1. Cool off. Each participant is ready to solve the problem.

2. Try steps 2-5 of "Handling the Problem Yourself" before seeking help.

3. Restate the problem. "I didn't like _____."

4. Brainstorm three to five solutions as a group and record them. Use the strategies worksheet.

5. Consider the consequences of each solution for both parties. Rate feelings + or - for both parties.

SOLUTIONS	CONSEQUENCES	ME + or -	OTHER + or -
1.			
2.			
3.			
4.			
5.			

6. Try a solution.

7. Report back to the group or assisting person.

Imaginary Mediation

TRANSFER

OBJECTIVE

Group members will write or draw about a mediation.

MATERIALS

Journal or paper, pencils, crayons, felt pens

PROCEDURE

The facilitator asks group members to think of a time two friends or two groups of friends were arguing. Ask them to remember what caused the conflict and how resolution was achieved. Next, members are asked to imagine they have been selected to be a mediator between two arguing people or groups of people. They use a real life situation or an imaginary one. Each mediation exercise includes any or all of the following:

1. Where does the meeting take place?
2. When does the meeting take place?
3. Would you have any guidelines?
4. What are your expectations?
5. Why did you choose a certain strategy
   for resolution?

Members are guided toward writing and/or drawing a picture about their mediation.

III. **PURPOSE** -- to present group members with methods for releasing unsettled feelings without involving others unnecessarily

One-Sided Conflict:
Brainstorming Session
AWARENESS

OBJECTIVE

Group members will brainstorm conflict situations in which one party doesn't perceive a problem exists.

MATERIALS

Chart paper, felt pen

PROCEDURE

The facilitator asks group members to think of a time when they've had a conflict with another person and that person did not perceive the problem. Members share these situations in a brainstorming session and record the conflicts on the chart paper. These situations are one-sided in that both parties do not see the situation as being a problem. Group members guess why the situation was one-sided and discuss how they sought to resolve the conflict within themselves.

Handling One-Sided Conflicts

PRACTICE

OBJECTIVE

Group members practice releasing blocked feelings in a safe manner.

MATERIALS

List from previous brainstorming activity

PROCEDURE

The facilitator brings the list of brainstormed situations from the previous awareness activity. A discussion follows to point out the frustration felt when both parties do not see that there is a problem needing resolution. When this occurs, there are several methods that can be used to provide release to the person perceiving the problem. Members discuss the use of the "Handling the Problem Yourself" model, altering the steps slightly. For example:

1. **COOL OFF --**
   Wait until the other person is ready to listen. Ask permission first.

2. **STATE THE PROBLEM --**
   "I don't like it when ...."

3. **STATE THE FEELING --**
   "I feel...when...."

4. **STATE WHAT YOU WISH WOULD HAPPEN --**
   "I wish that...."

5. **GIVE THANKS --**
   Thank the person for listening.

Group members take turns expressing their feelings as if they were actually talking to a person with whom they had a conflict. If desired, they contract with the group to deliver their feelings in person. Members are guided to consider that the goal in these one-sided situations is the release of blocked emotion. These emotional blocks can occur when one is not "heard" by another, as is the case in conflicts experienced by one party and denied by the other.

Role Playing One-Sided Conflicts
MORE PRACTICE

OBJECTIVE

Group members will learn role-play techniques as an alternate means of releasing angry feelings.

MATERIALS

Chair

PROCEDURE

The facilitator asks for a volunteer who is willing to share a one-sided conflict that has been experienced. The volunteer is asked to sit in a chair in the middle of the group. An empty chair is placed in front of the volunteer. There are several methods which can be used:

1. The volunteer talks to the chair as if the person with whom there was a conflict were actually sitting in that chair. The volunteer is urged to really voice the angry feelings. They might yell, raise voice, be dramatic, or otherwise express feeling. This helps release unwanted feelings and allows the volunteer to "let go" of the conflict.
2. The volunteer again talks to the empty chair as in the previous method. This time the volunteer also takes on the role of the person in the second chair. When the volunteer wants that person to speak, the participant moves to the empty chair and speaks to self, moving back to original chair when wanting to talk to conflicting person again, and so on. Basically, the volunteer imagines a conversation with the conflicting person by playing the role of both.
3. In the third method the volunteer asks a group member to play the part of the other party by sitting in the empty chair and responding like that person.

In a follow-up discussion, the effectiveness of these techniques is explored.

Adding Humor To a "No-Win" Situation

STILL MORE PRACTICE

OBJECTIVE

Group members will practice adding humor and exaggeration to a "no-win" situation.

MATERIALS

None

PROCEDURE

The facilitator introduces the idea that humor and exaggeration can provide release when persons are feeling up-tight or angry about a conflict. Members choose a situation which has caused conflict in their lives. Members become "actors," working together to turn the conflict into a melodrama. They are encouraged to be overly dramatic, using humor and exaggeration to diffuse some of the "heaviness" in the perceived conflict.

No Postage

TRANSFER

OBJECTIVE

Group members will write a humorous letter to a person with whom they have a conflict (with no intention of sending it).

MATERIALS

Journal or paper, pencil

PROCEDURE

The facilitator asks group members to think of a person with whom they have a one-sided conflict. Each writes a letter to that person exaggerating feelings about the conflict. Members know that they are writing this letter never to be mailed. The writing is used solely as a release for the person experiencing the conflict. Silliness, overstatement, and dramatizing are encouraged!

In the following chapter, "Sharing Ideas," group members refine their skills as listeners and speakers. They are guided to become clearer and more sophisticated with feedback and self-disclosure in the group. The communication skills gained enhance feelings of self-worth and open doors for easier cooperative efforts.

FACILITATOR LOG

Things to remember:

_____

_____

_____

_____

_____

_____

_____

_____

_____

_____

_____

_____

_____

_____

_____

_____

_____

_____

_____

_____

_____

Sharing
Ideas

Chapter 11

Sharing Ideas

The personal and social development of group members are enhanced by the feedback they give and receive and by their willingness to share information about themselves. Quality exchanges require both an active, reflective listener and a clear speaker. Constructive information is both nonthreatening and nonjudgmental. A distinction between constructive criticism and "barbs," "put-downs," or "killer statements" is made by group members in order for more meaningful exchanges to occur. What is fact and what is opinion, what is information and what is advice are important issues explored on the road to becoming a sophisticiated communicator. All of these topics are part of the following set of activities about "Sharing Ideas."

I. **PURPOSE** -- to emphasize the importance of active, reflective listening and clear speaking (NOTE: In this section it is important to do both awareness activities before moving ahead.)

Active Listening Characteristics
AWARENESS

OBJECTIVE

Group members will demonstrate the behavior characteristics of an active listener.

MATERIALS

Qualities of an Active Listener (Experience 11.1)

PROCEDURE

The facilitator leads a discussion of the components of active listening as presented on the following handout. The facilitator explains each quality, demonstrating appropriate eye contact, body language, and other aspects. Modeling is an essential component of learning appropriate listening skills. It is extremely important for the facilitator to show respect for the speaker and be genuinely interested in what is being said.

Group members form triads. Members are asked to choose the role of listener, speaker, or observer. There will be three timed sessions. The facilitator asks the speaker to choose a personal issue and talk for three to five minutes. During this time, the listener practices the qualities of an active listener as previously presented. The observer watches the listener and checks listening behaviors noted on the Active Listening sheet. At the end of the timed session, there is a two-minute sharing. Positions are traded until each member has had an opportunity to try each role.

If members have a difficult time choosing a talk topic, the following are suggested:

1. a memorable trip
2. a special friend
3. a hope for the future
4. an embarrassing moment

QUALITIES OF AN ACTIVE LISTENER

1. USE EYE CONTACT AND "LISTENING" BODY LANGUAGE

    -- look directly at speaker
    -- lean toward speaker
    -- nod head

2. PROVIDE ENCOURAGEMENT

    -- "Uh huh."
    -- "That sounds good."
    -- "Yes, I see what you mean."

3. LISTEN ATTENTIVELY

    -- remain silent when someone speaks
    -- give speaker complete attention

4. TELL BACK/PARAPHRASE

    -- "What I heard you say was...."

5. REFLECT FEELINGS

    -- "It sounds as if you're feeling...."
    -- "You sound...."

6. BE EMPATHETIC AND NONJUDGMENTAL

    -- value the speaker
    -- accept speaker's feelings
    -- forego judgments

Clear Speaking Techniques
MORE AWARENESS

OBJECTIVE

Group members will demonstrate behavior characteristics of a clear speaker.

MATERIALS

Clear Speaker Checklist (Experience 11.2)

PROCEDURE

The facilitator leads a discussion about clear speaking and its importance in the feedback process. The triad procedure from the previous awareness activity is repeated using topics such as:

1. a proud moment
2. a goal for the year
3. someone you admire
4. a fear you have

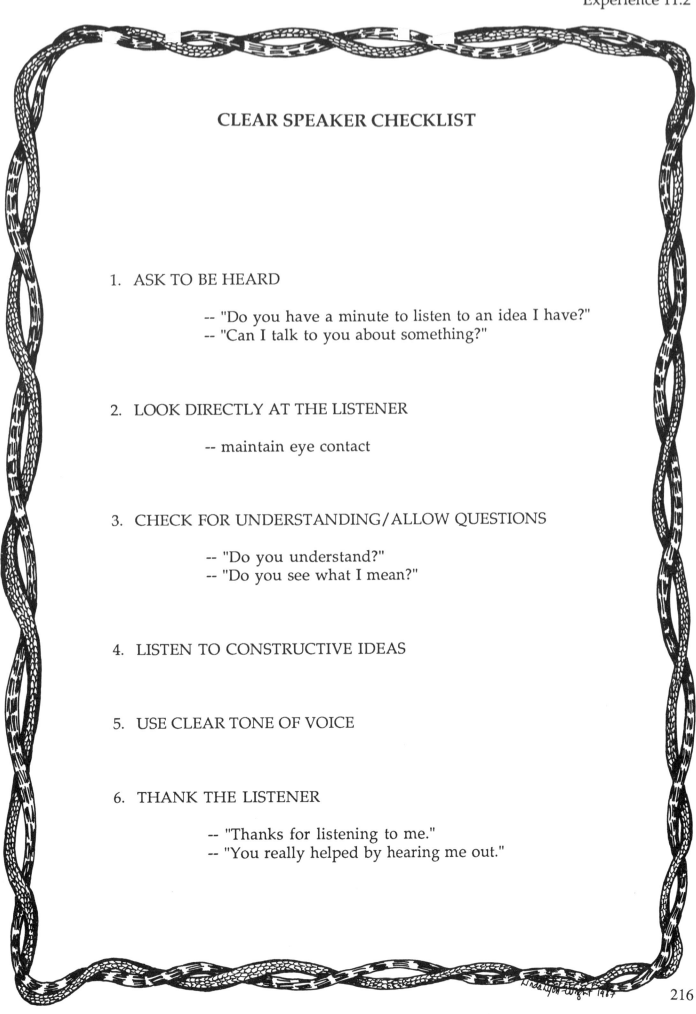

CLEAR SPEAKER CHECKLIST

1. ASK TO BE HEARD

   -- "Do you have a minute to listen to an idea I have?"
   -- "Can I talk to you about something?"

2. LOOK DIRECTLY AT THE LISTENER

   -- maintain eye contact

3. CHECK FOR UNDERSTANDING/ALLOW QUESTIONS

   -- "Do you understand?"
   -- "Do you see what I mean?"

4. LISTEN TO CONSTRUCTIVE IDEAS

5. USE CLEAR TONE OF VOICE

6. THANK THE LISTENER

   -- "Thanks for listening to me."
   -- "You really helped by hearing me out."

Practicing Active Listening

PRACTICE

OBJECTIVE

Group members will demonstrate active listening skills.

MATERIALS

Tape recorder, blank tape, video camera (if available)

PROCEDURE

The facilitator asks a volunteer to speak for approximately two minutes on any subject. The speaker's presentation is recorded and videotaped if possible. A group member who was listening then tells what was heard. The tape is played to compare what the listener thought was heard and what was actually said. The video is viewed to evaluate the body language of the active listeners, as well.

Do As I Say

MORE PRACTICE

OBJECTIVE

Group members will use clear verbal cues to direct others in completing a drawing.

MATERIALS

Drawing paper, felt pens

PROCEDURE

Group members are instructed to draw a simple, geometric design on a blank piece of paper. They are told that each is going to try to tell others how to draw what that person drew, so initial designs are kept secret. Members take turns using clear directions to tell others how to draw their pictures on blank pieces of paper. Speakers **may tell only and may not show**. Group members receiving directions are permitted to ask clarifying questions. A difficult variation involves not allowing questions from participants.

A follow-up discussion is held to reflect upon these questions:

1. Was it difficult to tell how to do your drawing?
2. What would have helped you get your directions across better?
3. Did the finished drawings look like yours?

Ideas On Listening

TRANSFER

OBJECTIVE

Group members will record perspectives on listening in their journals.

MATERIALS

Journals

PROCEDURE

The facilitator asks group members to copy the following open-ended sentences in their journals and complete them before the next session:

1. I am going to show _____ I am listening by _____.

2. When my parent doesn't listen to me, I feel _____.

3. When _____listens to what I say, I feel _____.

4. I wish _____ would listen to me _____.

5. I plan to listen better to _____ because _____.

Maze Mania

MORE TRANSFER

OBJECTIVE

Group members will practice giving clear directions to someone outside the group.

MATERIALS

Maze Mania (Experience 11.3), pencil

PROCEDURE

Members are asked to practice giving directions to a friend or family member. The facilitator gives the following directions to be carried out later:

Two people sit across from each other at a table. One person carefully directs a partner through the maze by giving clear directions and not showing. Questions for clarification are allowed or not allowed, depending upon the agreement made by the direction giver and receiver.

ENTER

EXIT

EXIT

Maze Mania

II. **PURPOSE** -- to clarify the difference between fact and opinion, information and advice, and to present a framework for delivering information (fact or opinion) in a nonthreatening, nonjudgmental manner

Fact Or Opinion?
Information Or Advice?
AWARENESS

OBJECTIVE

Group members will label statements as being fact or opinion, information or advice.

MATERIALS

Fact/Opinion, Information/Advice sheets (Experiences 11.4, 11.5)

PROCEDURE

The facilitator leads a discussion concerning the difference between fact and opinion: (1) "fact" is defined as something generally agreed to be true and (2) "opinion" is a viewpoint held to be true by one person or a particular group. The discussion moves next to considering information and advice: (1) "information," whether fact or opinion, is presented for consideration without requiring agreement or action by the receiver and (2) "advice," on the other hand, is wrought with "shoulds" and "oughts," whether stated or implied. Judgments, personal biases, and expectations exist with advice-giving and often block one's ability to hear what is said.

After discussing the above-mentioned distinctions, group members individually complete the appropriate level of "Fact/Opinion, Information/Advice" sheet (Experiences 11.4, 11.5). A discussion to compare conclusions and to discover "gray areas" serves as a follow-up.

FACT/OPINION -- INFORMATION/ADVICE
LEVEL I

MARK SENTENCES "F" FOR FACT OR "O" FOR OPINION.

_____ Friendships last forever.

_____ Teachers care about students.

_____ Reading is fun.

_____ Many children have parents who work outside the home.

_____ Many schools have after-school programs for students.

_____ Kids love animals.

_____ Some animals are in danger of becoming extinct.

_____ Flowering plants are alive.

_____ People love to swim.

MARK SENTENCES "I" FOR INFORMATION OR "A" FOR ADVICE.

_____ You ought to get a tutor.

_____ Some people have found tutors to be helpful.

_____ You should join a sports team instead of staying indoors so much.

_____ I hear Sandy is a good volleyball coach. It might be fun to join the team.

_____ You shouldn't eat so many sweets.

_____ My dentist suggested cutting down on candy or brushing more often.

_____ You ought to get a haircut. That long hair must be hard to wash.

_____ I found haircuts I like in this magazine.

_____ I've heard there are great exhibits at the fair this year.

_____ You need to get over your fear of crowds and come to the fair.

FACT/OPINION -- INFORMATION/ADVICE
LEVEL II

MARK SENTENCES "F" FOR FACT OR "O" FOR OPINION.

_____ You are your own best friend.

_____ Ours is a good country.

_____ Teachers care about students.

_____ Smoking is hazardous to your health.

_____ Depression is a feeling of deep sorrow.

_____ Dating is usually fun.

_____ Everyone loves to dance.

_____ Friends can be trusted.

_____ Cocaine is addictive.

_____ College is the best option after high school.

_____ 50-70% of all marriages end in divorce.

_____ Life is fun.

_____ Some people enjoy jogging.

_____ Swimming is the best form of exercise available.

_____ All people know how to read by the time they reach adulthood.

MARK SENTENCES "I" FOR INFORMATION OR "A" FOR ADVICE.

_____ You should follow "The Golden Rule."

_____ You might consider seeing a dietician or nutritionist about your stomach trouble.

_____ You should get to a doctor now.

_____ There is growing evidence linking depression and alcoholism.

_____ You should wait to get married until you're absolutely sure of your mate.

_____ Many parents want the best for their children.

_____ Go tell your family how you feel!

_____ You ought to care for your pets better by giving them daily vitamins.

_____ You would get better behavior from those children if you set firmer limits.

_____ Some children seem more comfortable knowing what others expect.

_____ If you read more and watched TV less, you'd have more to contribute to conversations.

_____ There is a wealth of information on that subject in the new science book series.

_____ Exercise would help you keep that weight off. You should join a health club.

_____ Everyone ought to have a job. No wonder you feel bored.

_____ Have you considered a job-training program?

Formats For Sharing

PRACTICE

OBJECTIVE

Group members will share information using "In my opinion," "One idea I have is...," or "Have you considered...." sentence formats.

MATERIALS

Role-Play sheets (Experiences 11.6, 11.7)

PROCEDURE

Group members listen to a role play between two volunteers. One presents a dilemma from Experience 11.6 or 11.7 and the other offers feedback. The respondent is guided to use the answering formats noted on the worksheet. The facilitator suggests to members that giving information in this way is less threatening, less judgmental and more easily heard by the receiver. "This-is-how-it-is" type responses aren't usually well received or helpful.

ROLE-PLAY SITUATIONS --- SHARING IDEAS
LEVEL I

1. My teacher always chooses me to answer questions in class. I like being called on, but the other kids make faces and say things about it.

    One idea I have is _____

    _____

    _____

    _____.

2. I really want to play the guitar, but my parents cannot afford the instrument. They said maybe in a few years I will be able to have lessons, but I'm ready now.

    In my opinion _____

    _____

    _____

    _____.

3. I have a hard time eating the hot lunches at school, but my dad thinks it's the best way for me to get a balanced meal. He works late and says it's easier for him to give me lunch money than to bother making lunches every day.

    Have you considered _____

    _____

    _____

    _____?

4. I'm really struggling in my reading group. Every time I get called on to read out loud I clam up. Part of our grade is for oral reading.

    Have you tried _____

    _____

    _____

    _____?

ROLE-PLAY SITUATIONS --- SHARING IDEAS
LEVEL II

1. One of my friends dislikes my other friends. She says it's either one or the other - my other friends or her.

   In my opinion _____

   _____

   _____

   _____.

2. My friend John laughs about my new boyfriend, who is very shy. I wish he liked my new boyfriend.

   Have you considered _____

   _____

   _____

   _____?

3. My mother has promised me a new wardrobe if I lose 20 pounds. I really don't want to diet right now. I'm not up for it. Still, I want to please my mother.

   One idea I have is _____

   _____

   _____

   _____.

4. I took extra break time once and now, almost a year later, my boss still brings it up every time I go for a break. She says, "Don't forget to check your watch!" It really upsets me.

   Have you tried _____

   _____

   _____

   _____?

"Killer Statements"

MORE PRACTICE

OBJECTIVE

Group members will offer constructive criticism stated in ways which avoid put-downs.

MATERIALS

Slips of paper, pencils, pens

PROCEDURE

The facilitator opens a discussion to determine what "constructive criticism" means and what purpose it serves. Group members are guided to see that useful criticism of someone's actions means simply pointing out in a gentle, positive manner how one can improve, strengthen, or benefit from constructive suggestions. When a person offering criticism does so with the intention of being helpful and encouraging, the suggestion is more easily heard. When offering criticism, it is important for group members to ask permission first and to point out the possible benefits of making certain behavior changes.

Frequently, critical comments are made without loving intention. These "killer statements" or put-downs are distinguished from constructive criticism in that they often attack the person involved and don't focus on behavior which can be changed. Group members are asked to write "killer statements" on the slips of paper provided, one per paper. The facilitator gives samples such as:

1. "How stupid can you get?"
2. "I cannot believe you did that!"
3. "Couldn't you think of anything else but that?"
4. "He thinks you're a jerk."

The "killer statements" are collected. Group members each draw one and take turns reading them to the group and telling how it would feel to have the comments really directed toward them. Members develop alternate ways of letting someone know a behavior change might be beneficial. They are guided to remember to: (1) ask permission, (2) focus on behavior which could be changed and the benefits of the change, and (3) make sure their intention is to be helpful. For example:

Killer statement: "Grow up, Carol!"

Constructive criticism: "Could I make a suggestion, Carol? **(permission)** Have you considered trying something other than crying? You could tell Janet she hurts your feelings when she teases you. **(behavior change)** She might stop teasing you if she really knew how much it affected you." **(possible benefit)**

230

Dear Katy
TRANSFER

OBJECTIVE

Group members will write useful information in response to a request for help.

MATERIALS

Journals, copy of Dear Katy! letters (Experiences 11.8, 11.9)

PROCEDURE

Group members are asked to write an opinion statement as if they were advice columnists. These are shared during the next session.

Dear Katy!
LEVEL I

Dear Katy,

My sister and I earn a weekly allowance for doing certain chores. I do mine; she doesn't do hers. We both still get the money. She promises to do better next week. Week after week she says this. I feel cheated. If I complain, she gets really angry with me. Help!

Fed Up in Los Angeles

Dear Fed Up,

One idea I have is _____

_____

_____

_____

_____.

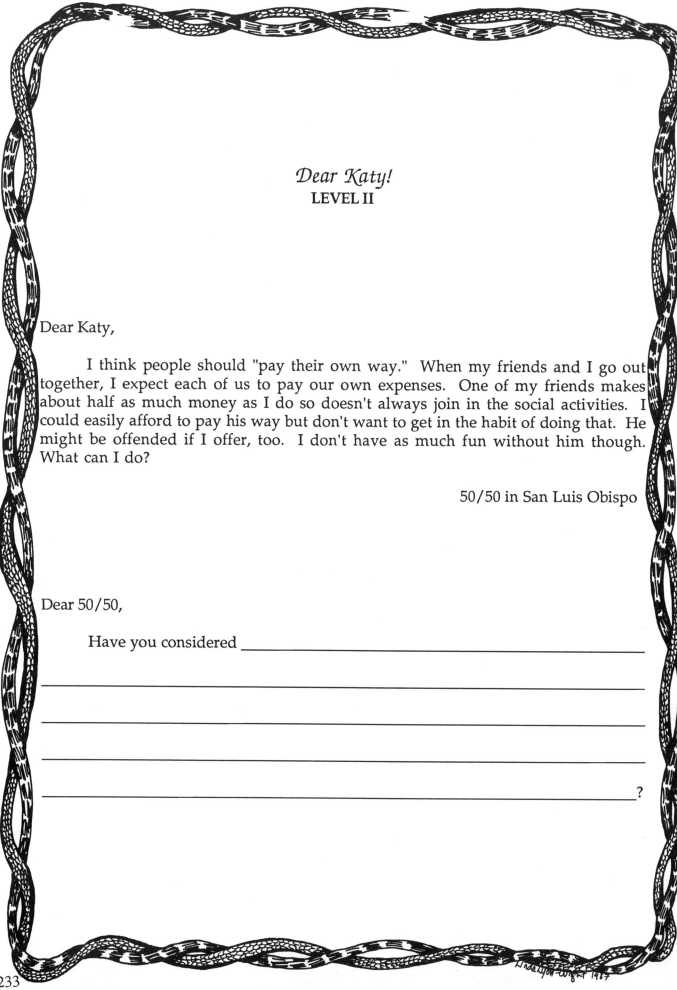

Dear Katy!
LEVEL II

Dear Katy,

I think people should "pay their own way." When my friends and I go out together, I expect each of us to pay our own expenses. One of my friends makes about half as much money as I do so doesn't always join in the social activities. I could easily afford to pay his way but don't want to get in the habit of doing that. He might be offended if I offer, too. I don't have as much fun without him though. What can I do?

50/50 in San Luis Obispo

Dear 50/50,

Have you considered _____

_____

_____

_____

_____?

III. **PURPOSE** -- to refine the information sharing skills of self-disclosure and feedback

Picture Window

AWARENESS

OBJECTIVE

Group members will create pictures, illustrating selected life events.

MATERIALS

12" X 18" drawing paper folded into quarters, colored pens

PROCEDURE

Members are asked to see the paper as a large window with four panes, each representing levels of self-awareness. The facilitator directs group members to draw pictures in each quadrant of the paper:

1. In the top left pane, draw a picture of something you know about yourself and everyone in the group knows as well.
2. In the bottom left pane, draw a picture of something you know about yourself and others don't know...a secret you have that you wouldn't mind sharing.
3. In the top right pane, draw a picture of what you think you would "see" if you were blind. Be creative!
4. In the bottom right pane, draw a picture of something unknown, such as a design, abstract sketch, or imagined patterns. In other words, draw a picture of something no one would recognize or know.

Group members discuss how everyone has secrets, blind spots (things they don't see in themselves), and possibilities completely unknown to them. The facilitator suggests that one way to tap into the wealth of opportunity in the "**unknown**" is to decrease the "**secrets**" area by telling trusted people important information about oneself (**self-disclosing**). In addition, people decrease their "**blind spots**" by accepting information coming to them from these trusted people (**feedback**).

My Window **

PRACTICE

OBJECTIVE

Group members will interact to disclose personal information and share feedback.

MATERIALS

My Window sheet (Experience 11.10), pencils, pens

PROCEDURE

Group members are given the My Window sheet (Experience 11.10) and are divided into groups of three or four. The groups are given the following instructions:

1. In the first window area write down something everyone knows about you. Check this out with your group partners. (**Arena**)

2. In the box beneath the first one, write a "secret" about yourself which you wouldn't mind sharing with the group. When this is done, share "secrets" in your triad. (**Facade**)

3. In your small group, ask permission from group members to give others in turn feedback about something you may know about them of which they may be unaware. Do this for everyone in the group in the form of a nature metaphor.

   For example, "Carl, may I share some information with you? When I watch you in group, I notice how carefully you choose your words. You remind me of a deer moving cautiously into a clearing in the woods." (**Blind Spot**)

   Write down what others say.

** Adapted from the Johari Window Model, Joseph Ingram and Harry Luft, as sited in *The 1973 Annual Handbook for Group Facilitators*, University Associates, 1973.

4. Spend a few minutes alone and write down something you learned about yourself that is important to you and to which you once were "blind."

   Examples:

   "When I was about seven, I realized my actions affected other people. Before that, I was sure no one even noticed me in my world."

   "Recently, I realized the divorce in my family had very little, if anything, to do with me. Before that, I was sure I had caused the split."

   Share these insights in your triad. (**Unknown**)

   In a follow-up discussion, group members share how it felt to participate in the experience. How easy/hard was it to share a secret? Did others have "blind spot" information of value to the receiver? The facilitator guides members to see that as facades and blind spots decrease in size, the arena becomes larger and less is unknown. This allows a person to function with more personal awareness and potency.

Variations on the "My Window" experience:

1. The directions for window #2 could be:

   Write down a secret on a slip of paper and put all secrets in the middle of the group. Draw one and read it as if it belonged to you. Tell how it feels to be keeping this secret and what might be gained by bringing it "out in the open."

2. The directions for window #3 could be:

   Ask for specific feedback instead of offering feedback in the form of metaphor. For example, "I want information about what is likeable about me."

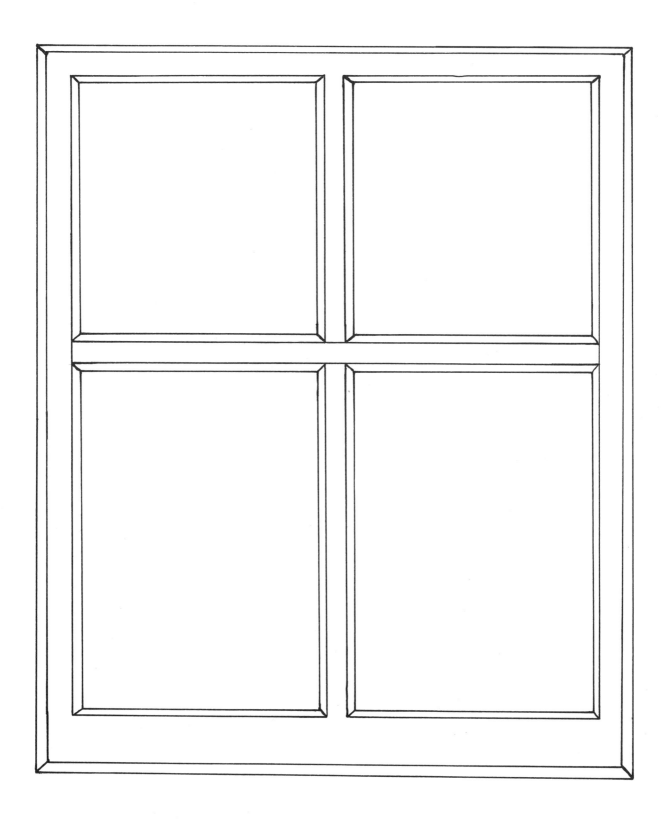

My Window

Secrets That I Keep

TRANSFER

OBJECTIVE

Group members will draw and/or write about secrets they keep.

MATERIALS

Journals, colored pens

PROCEDURE

Group members are asked to draw the outline of a human form to represent themselves. Inside the shape they are asked to draw a symbol for, or picture of, a secret they have. They are directed to draw this in the part of the body they imagine the secret is hidden, i.e., in the heart, in the stomach, in the head, mind, or some other area. Each is asked to write down the benefits of sharing the secret and getting information from others about it, as well as fears which keep the information hidden from others. Members are also asked to list safe people and places for divulging the information.

The skills acquired in this section, "Sharing Ideas", are refined during subsequent group meetings. Members share with more confidence and comfort as safety and trust are demonstrated and supported. Clear, easy communication, which is invaluable when conversing with new acquaintances and old friends, will be explored in depth in the next chapter, "Having Comfortable Conversations."

FACILITATOR LOG

Things to remember:

_____

_____

_____

_____

_____

_____

_____

_____

_____

_____

_____

_____

_____

_____

_____

_____

_____

_____

_____

_____

Having
Comfortable
Conversations

Linda Lyon-Wright 1987

Chapter 12

Having Comfortable Conversations

Throughout People Skills experiences practiced in *BELONGING*, participants have worked to expand their repertoire of interactive skills. These skills are called upon in this section as group members are encouraged to interact for longer periods of time with increasing numbers of people. Each situation brings its own set of challenges. The facilitator's role in "Having Comfortable Conversations" is that of support person, always there to assure someone's success by cuing individuals or interjecting humor. The following activities are designed to ease group members into conversational settings. Expectations are progressively more complex, yet members are assured of enjoyable, rewarding outcomes.

I. **PURPOSE** -- to guide group members into conversations with themselves in preparation for talking with others

Body Talk
AWARENESS

OBJECTIVE

Group members will carry on a conversation with a selected part of their bodies, i.e., hair, eyes, hands, ears, or other part.

MATERIALS

Paper, pencils, pens

PROCEDURE

Group members are asked to select a part of the body with which to have a conversation. They write out the dialogue in the form of a play. The facilitator writes out guiding questions to help with the experience:

1. What are you and how are you today?
2. What makes you happy? What do you like to do?
3. What do you dislike? What causes you to feel badly?
4. What do you want to know from me?
5. Can you think of something we can do together?

Group members come back together to read the dialogues. A variation is to have pairs of people read each dialogue, taking separate parts. The facilitator encourages humor and also points out important information the body has for each person.

Interview You

PRACTICE

OBJECTIVE

Group members will interview themselves as a means of gaining interactive skill.

MATERIALS

Interview You! sheet (Experience 12.1), pencils

PROCEDURE

Group members move to quiet, private corners and ask themselves the questions on the "Interview You!" sheet (Experience 12.1). The group rejoins to share results (if desired) after 10-15 minutes. The facilitator asks:

1. Did you learn anything new about yourself?
2. How did it feel to do the exercise?
3. Could you use this form to interview a group member?

The next session can be used to interview another group member by using the same interview sheet.

INTERVIEW YOU!

What are your name and age? _____

_____

_____

Describe yourself physically. _____

_____

_____

Tell me about your strengths and weaknesses._____

_____

_____

I'd like to hear about your friends and family. _____

_____

_____

Please talk about the most memorable experience of your life. Who was there?
How did you feel? _____

_____

_____

_____

_____

Letter Exchange

TRANSFER

OBJECTIVE

Group members will write letters to and from themselves, thus carrying on both ends of a conversation.

MATERIALS

Journals, pencils, pens

PROCEDURE

Group members are asked to write a brief letter to themselves similar to the following example:

> Dear Self,
>
> I'm pretty happy today. I'm earning money to go to the fair in August. That's one of my favorite events each year. I really can't wait! What's been happening with you? Write soon.
>
> Love, Susan

After this, members are instructed to respond to the letter, using the following guide:

> Dear Susan,
>
> I'm happy when you're happy. Fairs with all the food, rides, and exhibits are so much fun! How neat it is that you figured out some way to earn money to go. I've been waiting for a chance to relax and read instead of so much work, though. Can you help?
>
> Love,
> Your Self

These exchanges can continue indefinitely as each ends with a question to be considered. The facilitator emphasizes that this is a great way to check in with oneself, as well as a way to learn conversation skills.

II. **PURPOSE** -- to guide group members into conversations with one or two other people

Turtle Talk
AWARENESS

OBJECTIVE

Group members will create pictures which include information about themselves to serve as "cue cards" in conversation.

MATERIALS

Turtle Talk drawings (Experience 12.2), colored pens

PROCEDURE

Group members write their names on the head of the turtle picture. In each of the sections of the turtle shell, members write or draw some of the following information:

1. something they do especially well
2. something they avoid doing
3. three words that describe them well
4. three words that describe a close friend
5. places they remember well
6. how they felt doing this experience

Group members are encouraged to decorate their turtles in unique ways. When all turtle drawings are completed and decorated, members choose a partner. Members of each dyad take turns talking about themselves for three to five minutes-at which time the facilitator calls "switch" or "stop." The listener in the dyad is encouraged to ask questions. Groups of three different people are formed next, with the same procedure followed.

Turtle Talk

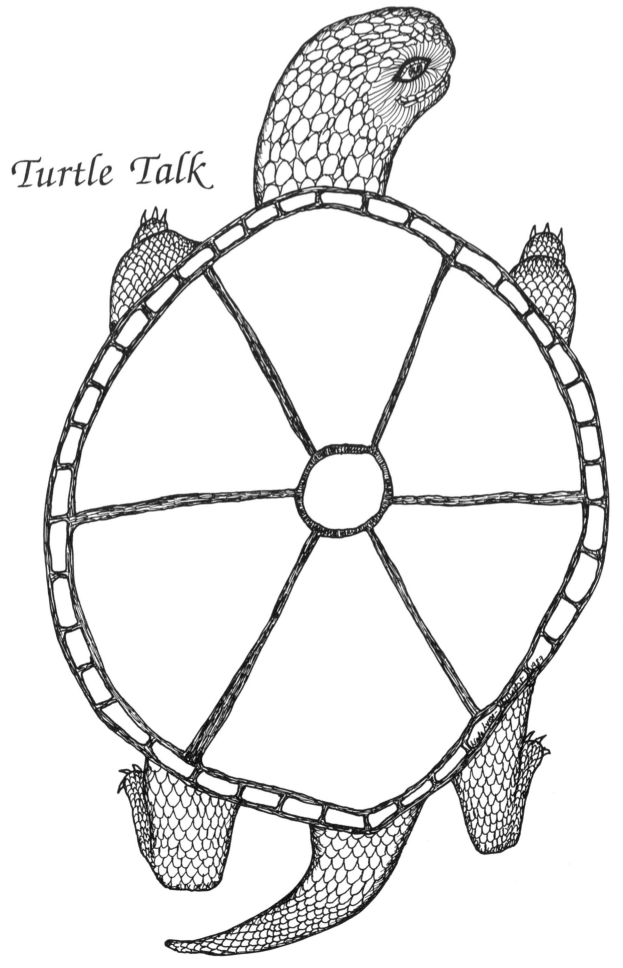

Video Buzz Sessions

PRACTICE

OBJECTIVE

Group members will engage in "cued" conversations while being videotaped.

MATERIALS

Video camera and monitor, cue cards, props

PROCEDURE

The facilitator sets up video equipment and any props prior to the group meeting. Group members are asked to pair off and volunteer to be taped while conversing. The facilitator holds up cue cards throughout the three to five minute interchange and creates new cues to prompt, according to the flow of the conversation. Scenes can be set up to be humorous or serious. Some scene, cue card, and prop suggestions include:

1. Scene: A first meeting at a party

    Cues:
    -- Introductions
    -- What do you do? Where do you work or go to school?
    -- How do you know the host (hostess)?
    -- Create new ones as conversation develops.

    Props: Food, couch, or chairs

2. Scene: Sitting together at a sports event

    Cues:
    -- Introductions
    -- Who are you rooting for?
    -- Do you come to games often?
    -- Offer popcorn.
    -- Who are your favorite players?
    -- Create new cues as conversation develops. Add humorous
       possibilities.

Props: Two chairs and popcorn

3. Scene: Friends discussing a problem one is
             having

    Cues:
         -- How are you feeling?
         -- What's going on?
         -- How can I help?
         -- Have you tried...?
         -- Invitation to do something together
         -- Create other possibilities.

    Props: Table and chairs, tea or snacks

Group members watch the video during the next session and discuss the quality of
the listening and speaking seen. They are asked to consider how each can encourage
the conversation of the other.

Fantasy Friend

TRANSFER

OBJECTIVE

Group members will write a fantasy dialogue with an imaginary friend.

MATERIALS

Journals, pens

PROCEDURE

Group members are instructed to take a few moments at home and draw a picture of an imaginary friend-this could be a human friend or a creation! Next, participants create a conversation between themselves and the fantasy friends. Members are encouraged to say anything at all in the conversation-to be funny, loose, and free. The facilitator gives members the opportunity to share these fantasy interchanges during the next group meeting.

III. **PURPOSE** -- to encourage group members to try a variety of roles in groups

The Group And Me
AWARENESS

OBJECTIVE

Group members will practice a nonverbal exercise to learn the importance of equal exchange in a group.

MATERIALS

Nerf or other soft ball, Nonverbal Situation Cards (Experience 12.3)

PROCEDURE

Group members are asked to sit in a circle and face each other. The situation cards are passed out until all are used. Some members may have more than one card. The ball is tossed freely around the circle. When the ball is thrown to the one with card #1, that person acts out what the card says by using the ball. The action is stopped and a discussion ensues as to what happens in a group discussion when similar behaviors occur. After this discussion, the ball is again thrown freely back and forth among members until the person holding card #2 catches it. The procedure continues until all cards have been used.

NONVERBAL SITUATION CARDS

1. Hold the ball and throw it up and down in the air. **Don't** pass it on to anyone else.

2. Point to one other person. Throw the ball back and forth between the two of you, ignoring the others.

3. Act like the facilitator and indicate by pointing that the ball must go from person to person around the circle.

4. Pass the ball to someone else. When that person passes it on, reach over and grab it.

5. Point to two other people. Indicate that the ball will only be thrown among the three of you.

6. Act like the facilitator and pass the ball to someone, indicating it must come back to you. Each person you throw to must return the ball to you. You are the only one who can pass the ball to a new person.

7. Hold the ball. Then throw it over your head so that it lands behind you, outside the group.

8. Hold the ball. Slowly look at each person. After you have had eye contact with everyone, carefully select someone and throw the ball to that member.

Task Discussions

PRACTICE

OBJECTIVE

Group members will actively participate in a discussion in one to three different capacities.

MATERIALS

Discussion Task Cards (Experience 12.4)

PROCEDURE

The facilitator chooses a topic for the group to discuss. Suggestions are

1. the importance of friendship
2. why society needs rules
3. shyness: ways to overcome it
4. experiences members have had with feelings such as joy, sorrow, fear, anger
5. why vacations are important
6. how you feel about being the youngest, middle, or oldest child in your family

Members choose their own topics, as well. Group members are given two Discussion Task Cards (Experience 12.4). Members are to respond in group discussion according to the actions described on their cards.

The facilitator, who participates in the discussion, serves as a role model and practices all roles listed on the task cards.

Follow-up discussion:

1. Did you feel confined being able to respond only as directed on your task cards?
2. Were you able to tell what roles others played?
3. What did you like or dislike about this experience?
4. Would you like to try this again and draw new cards?

DISCUSSION TASK CARDS

1. You present a personal viewpoint frequently during the discussion.

    -- "In my opinion...."
    -- "I feel that...."

2. You question those presenting ideas.

    -- "Why do you feel that?"
    -- "How can that be?"
    -- "Where did you get that information?"
    -- "What makes you say that?"

3. You are an active listener, who periodically repeats what has been said.

    -- "What I heard you say was...."

4. You are a reflective listener and give feedback on information heard.

    -- "It sounds like...."

5. You keep things "on track," not letting members talk about something else.

    -- "You're getting off the topic we selected."
    -- "That's interesting, but we're supposed to be
       talking about...."

6. You are a reflective listener and give feedback as to the feelings behind someone's words.

    -- "It sounds as if you feel...."

Interviewing A Partner

MORE PRACTICE

OBJECTIVE

Group members will interview each other and share information learned with the group.

MATERIALS

Interview Questions (Experience 12.5)

PROCEDURE

The facilitator passes out an "Interview Questions" sheet (Experience 12.5) to all members and asks them to think of someone they would like to interview-perhaps someone not known well. Members break into pairs and begin interviewing each other. A follow-up group discussion is held to share information learned about group participants.

Linda Lyon-Wright 1987

INTERVIEW QUESTIONS

1. What is your full name?

_____

2. Who lives with you at home?

_____

3. What do you enjoy doing in your spare time?

_____

4. Do you have any plans for the weekend?

_____

5. If you could be anyone, who would it be?

_____

6. Who was one of your favorite teachers? Why?

_____

7. Where is your favorite place to visit?

_____

8. What is a secret wish that you have?

_____

Independent Conversations

TRANSFER

OBJECTIVE

Group members will engage in a discussion with someone outside of group.

MATERIALS

Journal, pencil

PROCEDURE

The facilitator asks group members to strike up a conversation with one or more persons before the next group meeting. Members are encouraged to talk to someone they do not know well.

The facilitator asks members to log their conversation and attempt to define how they participated: What did you talk about? Was it easy or difficult? Did the other person appear interested in what you were saying?

FACILITATOR LOG

Things to remember:

Beginning Again . . .

BELONGING holds the collective energies of everyone who has contributed to its birth. All have been expecting a logical ending to make itself known. Not so. The process of becoming who we truly are brings forth infinite, ever-changing possibilities. The human journey we share is one of constant creation and recreation. We grow and access more of the essential strength, beauty, and clarity of purpose which exist at the core of each of us, patiently awaiting our "aha!" moment of recognition. When acknowledged, this essence is free to burst forth and diminish the tedium of blindly repeating old patterns. We allow ourselves to shine as brightly as jewels in the night sky.

Carry on.

INDEX